Famous Hands from Famous Matches

MAXWELL MACMILLAN BRIDGE SERIES

Publishing Editor: Glyn Liggins

In this series:
REESE, T.
Brilliancies and Blunders
in the European Bridge Championship

In preparation:
FLINT, J. & NORTH, F.
Tiger Bridge Revisited

SENIOR, B.
Bread and Butter Bidding

SMITH, N.
Bridge Literature

CROWHURST, E.
Acol — The Complete System

HACKETT, P.
Bridge Around the World

A full catalogue of Maxwell Macmillan Bridge books is available from:
Maxwell Macmillan Bridge
London Road, Wheatley, Oxford OX9 1YR

Famous Hands
from Famous Matches

by Terence Reese
&
David Bird

MAXWELL MACMILLAN BRIDGE

MAXWELL MACMILLAN INTERNATIONAL PUBLISHING GROUP

EUROPE/ MIDDLE EAST/AFRICA	Maxwell Macmillan International, Hollow Way, Cowley, Oxford OX4 2YH, England Tel: (0865) 748754 Fax: (0865) 748808
U.S.A.	Macmillan Publishing Company 866 Third Avenue, New York, NY 10022 Tel: (212) 702-2000 Fax: (212) 605-9341
CANADA	1200 Eglinton Avenue East, Suite 200, Don Mills, Ontario M3C 3N1, Canada Tel: (416) 449-6030 Fax: (416) 449-0068
AUSTRALIA/ NEW ZEALAND	Lakes Business Park, Building A1, 2 Lord Street, Botany, NSW 20119, Australia Tel: (02) 316-9444 Fax: (02) 316-9485
ASIA/PACIFIC (Except Japan)	72 Hillview Avenue, 103-00 Tacam House, Singapore 2366 Tel: (65) 769-6000 Fax: (65) 769-3731
LATIN AMERICA	28100 US Highway 19 North, Suite 200, Clearwater, FL 34621 Tel: (813) 725-4033 Fax: (813) 725-2185
JAPAN	8th Floor, Matsuoka Central Building, 1-7-1 Nishishinjuku, Shinjuku-Ku, Tokyo 160, Japan Tel: 81-3-3344-5201 Fax: 81-3-3344-5202

First edition 1991

Library of Congress Cataloging in Publication Data Applied for

Cataloguing in Publication Data can be obtained from the British Library

ISBN 1 85744 501 5

Cover design by Pintail, Dalrymple, Ayrshire
Typeset by Lands Services, East Molesey and
Printed in Great Britain by BPCC Wheatons Ltd, Exeter

Contents

In the sixty odd years of tournament bridge there
have been innumerable brilliant, disastrous,
or mirth-provoking deals. The authors describe
some of the brightest and best, including at least one
that led to murder.
Many of the deals are clever, but not heavyweight:
they touch on the history and humour of the game.
In every case the scene is set on the first of two pages
and the reader is asked:
What do you suppose happened next?

Part 1
Early Days

Thanks mainly to Culbertson's genius for publicity,
1930 to 1940 was an era of great matches, at first
between pairs and later between teams.

Eyes of the World

It is slightly sad, in a way, to recall the Culbertson–Lenz 'Bridge Battle of the Century' in 1931. Culbertson had just published the Blue Book and was confident that he could knock out the old school, represented by Sidney Lenz, in whose 1–2–3 system opening bids of two were strong and bids of three were forcing.

The match was played in a glare of publicity such as never has attended any other bridge game nor ever will again. The day-by-day scores were front-page news in 30 countries and every move was reported on the radio. You can imagine how the press enjoyed the following deal.

Love all; Dealer East.

```
              ♠ A K 2
              ♡ Q 8
              ♢ J 7 3
              ♣ K J 8 7 5
♠ 7 5                          ♠ Q 10 9 8 6 4 3
♡ J 6 5 4 2       N            ♡ A 10 7
♢ Q 10 6 4     W   E           ♢ 9 8
♣ 10 3            S            ♣ 6
              ♠ J
              ♡ K 9 3
              ♢ A K 5 2
              ♣ A Q 9 4 2
```

West	North	East	South
Ely	*Sidney*	*Josephine*	*Oswald*
Culbertson	*Lenz*	*Culbertson*	*Jacoby*
		Pass	1♣
Pass	3♣	3♠	4♠
Pass	5♣	Pass	6♣
All Pass			

What actually happened, we will see in a moment. The question is: can South make six clubs on a trump lead?

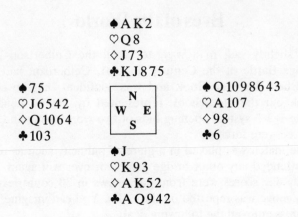

```
            ♠ A K 2
            ♡ Q 8
            ◇ J 7 3
            ♣ K J 8 7 5
♠ 7 5          ┌─────┐      ♠ Q 10 9 8 6 4 3
♡ J 6 5 4 2    │  N  │      ♡ A 10 7
◇ Q 10 6 4   W │     │ E    ◇ 9 8
♣ 10 3         │  S  │      ♣ 6
               └─────┘
            ♠ J
            ♡ K 9 3
            ◇ A K 5 2
            ♣ A Q 9 4 2
```

Jacoby said in his commentary that after his partner's jump raise — obviously a big bid in his system — he decided to go for a slam in any case and bid four spades in the hope of averting a spade lead.

The question never arose, because Mrs Culbertson led the ace of hearts out of turn. In those days declarer could call for the lead of a specified suit. Jacoby requested a diamond lead and had no problem when the jack held.

It was assumed at the time that a spade or club lead would have broken the contract, but that is not necessarily so. After drawing trumps the declarer leads a low heart from dummy and East must duck. When the king of spades wins South throws a heart on the second spade, ruffs a spade, cashes the ace and king of diamonds and exits with a heart, leaving East on play.

A Tactical Withdrawal

The Lenz–Jacoby partnership led for the first 43 of the 150 rubbers match, but then a decline set in. There was a famous hand where Lenz was beguiled by his holding of four aces into bidding no-trumps three times in succession, despite a 4–1–4–4 distribution. Seven spades was on, but the suit (♠AQ103 opposite ♠KJ74) was never mentioned and the partnership played in seven hearts with seven to the queen-jack opposite a singleton ace.

A further calamity, on a more normal hand, occurred on this deal:

Game all, North-South 35; Dealer East.

```
                    ♠ 106
                    ♡ Q86
                    ◊ KQ9743
                    ♣ 103
    ♠ K5                          ♠ Q9873
    ♡ KJ42         N              ♡ 95
    ◊ J5         W   E            ◊ A86
    ♣ QJ954        S              ♣ 876
                    ♠ AJ42
                    ♡ A1073
                    ◊ 102
                    ♣ AK2
```

West	North	East	South
Sidney	Josephine	Oswald	Ely
Lenz	Culbertson	Jacoby	Culbertson
		Pass	1♣
Pass	2◊	Pass	2NT
All Pass			

Two no-trumps was a game bid, as North-South had 35 below and the first trick in no-trumps counted 35.

West led the queen of clubs and South won the second round, East having played the seven and the eight. Then a diamond to the king, heart to the ace, diamond to the queen and ace. What do you suppose happened then?

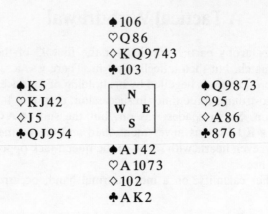

```
              ♠106
              ♡Q86
              ◇KQ9743
              ♣103
   ♠K5          ┌─────────┐      ♠Q9873
   ♡KJ42        │   N     │      ♡95
   ◇J5          │ W   E   │      ◇A86
   ♣QJ954       │   S     │      ♣876
                └─────────┘
              ♠AJ42
              ♡A1073
              ◇102
              ♣AK2
```

Playing in two no-trumps, a game bid, Culbertson won the second club, played a diamond to the king, a heart to the ace, and another diamond to the queen and ace.

Now Jacoby, who had played the seven and eight of clubs on the first two rounds, judged that another club would not beat two no-trumps. The declarer would lose just three clubs, a diamond and a heart. So he switched to the three of spades. This lost to the king, but now Lenz returned a spade, since he imagined that South still held ace-six of clubs.

Jacoby's spade switch was high-class play, but a modern player would have led the nine rather than the three, indicating that he did not wish to have the suit returned.

When two no-trumps was made, Lenz started the offensive and his criticisms were not well received, Jacoby observing that he had made a play that only twelve experts in the country would understand, and unfortunately Mr Lenz did not appear, at that particular moment, to be one of them.

Jacoby withdrew after the 103rd rubber and was replaced by one Commander Winfield Liggett. 'Lig', as his partner called him, seems to have played quite well, but the Culbertsons, who had been over 20,000 up at one time, finally won by 8,980.

Harry's All-Round Hand

The 1934 Schwab Trophy match, between England and the USA, was played at London's Dorchester Hotel. This was one of several sensational deals:

```
         ♠ J 10 9 8 7
         ♡ J
         ◇ A 10 3
         ♣ K J 10 4
         ┌─────────┐
         │    N    │
         │  W   E  │
         │    S    │
         └─────────┘
         ♠ K
         ♡ Q 10 7 6 5 4 3 2
         ◇ J 7
         ♣ 7 2
```

West	North	East	South
Culbertson	*Hughes*	*Lightner*	*Ingram*
	1♠	Pass	Pass [1]
Double	Pass	Pass	2◇ [2]
Double	Pass	Pass	2♡
Double	All Pass		

[1] North-South were playing a strong club system, so the opening was limited.
[2] A psychic call straight from the Upper Fourth.

Before bidding two hearts Harry Ingram spent some moments considering a further psyche, to be followed by three hearts. Eventually, noting that the score was Love All (so that a big penalty might not show sufficient profit), he bid just two hearts. To his surprise, this was doubled.

Culbertson, sitting West, led the two of spades to East's ace and the five of spades was returned. How would you plan the play?

These were the four hands:

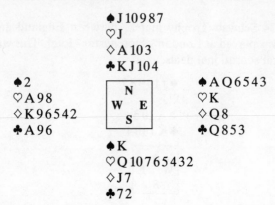

```
                    ♠J10987
                    ♡J
                    ◇A103
                    ♣KJ104
    ♠2                              ♠AQ6543
    ♡A98          N                ♡K
    ◇K96542     W     E            ◇Q8
    ♣A96          S                ♣Q853
                    ♠K
                    ♡Q10765432
                    ◇J7
                    ♣72
```

West led the two of spades to the ace and a low spade was returned. Ingram, flushed with his success in the bidding, made the careless play of ruffing this trick. He was overruffed and went one down. Had he discarded a diamond instead, he would have made the contract.

Culbertson, furious at being psyched, demanded to know why North had not put his partner back to three diamonds! He then turned on Ingram. "How dare you hesitate before bidding two hearts?" he demanded. His protest, an absurd one, was later withdrawn.

In the other room the bidding was unbelievably bad:

West	North	East	South
Lederer	*Morehead*	*Rose*	*Mrs Culbertson*
	Pass	Pass	3♡
4◇	4♠	5◇	Pass
Pass	Double	All Pass	

The merits of a double of four spades apparently escaped the East player. Five diamonds doubled went down 500.

8

A Trick Each Way

In 1935 Mike Gottlieb and Howard Schenken, members of the team described as the Four Aces, played a match of 100 rubbers against Harry Ingram and Stan Hughes. They were stronger than any of the Culbertson partnerships and won by a fair margin, though they had the worse of the following deal:

North-South game; Dealer East.

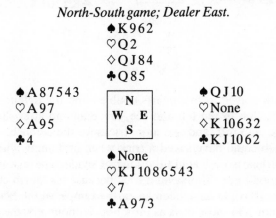

♠K962
♡Q2
◇QJ84
♣Q85

♠A87543
♡A97
◇A95
♣4

♠QJ10
♡None
◇K10632
♣KJ1062

♠None
♡KJ10 86543
◇7
♣A973

Herbert Newmark was deputising for Hughes in this session and the bidding went:

West	North	East	South
Newmark	*Schenken*	*Ingram*	*Gottlieb*
		Pass	Pass
1♠	Pass	3♠	4♡
4♠	Double	Pass	5♡
Double	All Pass		

West led his singleton club to the ten and ace. Declarer played a heart to the queen and when Newmark won the next heart he underled his ace of diamonds. Ingram returned a low club for his partner to ruff and the defence made two more club tricks, for 800. Do you see how either side might have done better?

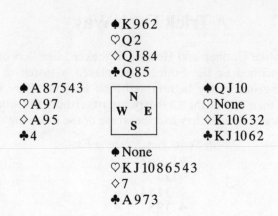

```
                  ♠ K962
                  ♡ Q2
                  ♦ QJ84
                  ♣ Q85
    ♠ A87543          N          ♠ QJ10
    ♡ A97         W     E        ♡ None
    ♦ A95            S           ♦ K10632
    ♣ 4                          ♣ KJ1062
                  ♠ None
                  ♡ KJ1086543
                  ♦ 7
                  ♣ A973
```

Something this page. South played in five hearts doubled and the defence was excellent: club to the ten and ace, low diamond after the ace of hearts, club ruff, and two more tricks for the defence.

Gottlieb could have saved a trick when in dummy with the queen of hearts by leading the king of spades and discarding his diamond loser. This saves a trick because his fourth club is a winner. It would have been an early example of the Scissors Coup, known in those days as the Coup Without a Name.

Anything else? Well, if we are to be *extremely* critical, West could have averted the coup by going up with the ace of hearts on the first round and leading his low diamond. You didn't see that, admit it!

A Successful Diversion

In 1937 another big match was played, this time at the Waldorf Hotel between the Austrian team that had won the European Championship and a more or less self-selected team consisting of Konstam and Mathieson, Harrison-Gray and Merkin, with Ewart Kempson as fifth man. As expected, the Austrians, headed by the legendary combination of Schneider and Jellinek, were too good for the home team.

Big crowds attended every session at the Waldorf Hotel. The most publicised deal was the following:

Game all; Dealer North.

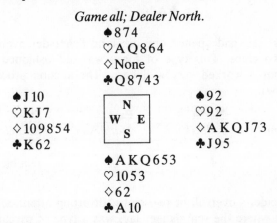

```
              ♠874
              ♡AQ864
              ◇None
              ♣Q8743
  ♠J10                      ♠92
  ♡KJ7          N          ♡92
  ◇109854    W   E         ◇AKQJ73
  ♣K62          S          ♣J95
              ♠AKQ653
              ♡1053
              ◇62
              ♣A10
```

Never one to hold back when he had a bit of distribution, Gray opened one heart on the North hand and the bidding continued:

West	North	East	South
Herbert	*Gray*	*Bludhorn*	*Merkin*
	1♡	2◇	3♠
4◇	Pass	Pass	4♠
Pass	5◇(!)	Pass	5♠
All Pass			

West led a low club to the jack and ace and twelve tricks were made.

At the other table North passed and Mathieson, East, opened one diamond. What do you suppose Schneider bid on the South cards?

11

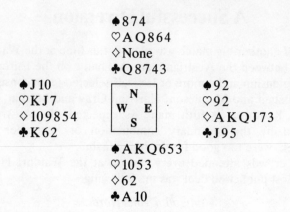

```
              ♠874
              ♡AQ864
              ◇None
              ♣Q8743
  ♠J10          ┌─────┐      ♠92
  ♡KJ7          │  N  │      ♡92
  ◇109854       │W   E│      ◇AKQJ73
  ♣K62          │  S  │      ♣J95
               └─────┘
              ♠AKQ653
              ♡1053
              ◇62
              ♣A10
```

After East had opened one diamond Schneider overcalled
with two clubs. This type of foray was old-fashioned even
then, but it worked very well here. The auction proceeded
as follows:

West	North	East	South
Konstam	*Jellinek*	*Mathieson*	*Schneider*
	Pass	1◇	2♣
2NT	3♣	3NT	Double
All Pass			

Schneider's overcall of two clubs, diverting attention from
the suit where the real danger lay, was a type of psychic not
uncommon in Auction days. Here the cards combined in a
devilish way to assist him, both East and West pushing forward
on the strength of the same feature. A club was led and the
defence took the first nine tricks for a penalty of 1400.

Herbert's Fourth Choice

This is another deal from the match at the Waldorf Hotel between the Austrian team that had beaten 'the Culbertsons' and a British team. It was exciting at both tables.

Game all; Dealer West.

```
              ♠ A 10
              ♡ J 8 7 6 2
              ◇ A 6 2
              ♣ 1 0 5 2
♠ Q 9 7 6 5                    ♠ 8 3
♡ K Q 10 9 5 3    N           ♡ A 4
◇ None         W     E         ◇ J 9 8 7 4
♣ 9 4             S            ♣ K J 8 6
              ♠ K J 4 2
              ♡ None
              ◇ K Q 10 5 3
              ♣ A Q 7 3
```

West	North	East	South
Mathieson	*Bludhorn*	*Konstam*	*Herbert*
3♡	Pass	4♡	4♠ [1]
Double [2]	Pass	Pass	4 NT
Pass	Pass	Double	5♣
Pass	Pass	Double	5◇
Pass	Pass	Double	All Pass

[1] Nowadays South would double, trusting partner to take appropriate action.
[2] As it turned out, he would have done better to pass, but one can easily imagine circumstances where the double would have been right.

East's double of five diamonds must have looked the best thing since Grandma died, but disillusionment was in store. How do you suppose the play went?

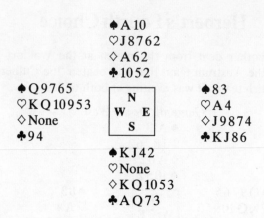

<pre>
                      ♠ A 10
                      ♡ J 8 7 6 2
                      ◇ A 6 2
                      ♣ 1 0 5 2
    ♠ Q 9 7 6 5   N   ♠ 8 3
    ♡ K Q 10 9 5 3   W   E   ♡ A 4
    ◇ None   S   ◇ J 9 8 7 4
    ♣ 9 4   ♣ K J 8 6
                      ♠ K J 4 2
                      ♡ None
                      ◇ K Q 10 5 3
                      ♣ A Q 7 3
</pre>

Declarer ruffed the heart lead and took an immediate finesse of the ten of spades. He then cashed the ace of spades and finessed the queen of clubs successfully. After playing the ace of clubs he led the king of spades, discarding dummy's last club. East ruffed and returned a trump but declarer could win with the ten of diamonds, ruff a club, ruff a heart and ruff a club with the ace. That was nine tricks in the bag and he still had the king and queen of diamonds to come.

This was the bidding in the other room.

West	North	East	South
Schneider	*Merkin*	*Jellinek*	*Gray*
Pass	Pass	Pass	1 ◇
1 ♡	Double	Pass	1 ♠
Pass	3 ◇	Pass	3 ♡
Pass	3 NT	Pass	5 ◇
Pass	Pass	Double	All Pass

There are two points of interest in the auction. Firstly, North's penalty double of one heart was poorly judged. Why should he want to make hearts trumps when he knows there is a stack of hearts to his right? Nowadays such doubles are more usefully employed for take-out (in tournament play, at any rate) and North would make the more sensible call of one no-trump.

Secondly, it seems that Gray had no reason to remove three no-trumps, which would have been easy enough. His partner's earlier double had suggested strength in hearts, which would be of little value in a suit contract. Gray went one down in five diamonds, taking the spade finesse the wrong way.

Part 2

Well Played, Sir — and Madam

Every big tournament has its Brilliancy Prize
nowadays, but these examples from earlier times
stand well by comparison.

Language Problem

Britain won the European Championship at Montreux in 1954 and the same team was chosen for the world championship match in New York the following year. The match was close for most of the way, but the British team lasted better. An instructive point on this deal, fairly late in the match, was not noted by the commentators:

East-West game; Dealer East.

```
                 ♠ A 6 3
                 ♡ Q 10 7 3
                 ◇ K 7 2
                 ♣ A 8 3
  ♠ K J 5                        ♠ 10 9 7 2
  ♡ J 9 6        ┌─────┐         ♡ 8 5 2
  ◇ Q 10 5 3     │  N  │         ◇ J 9
  ♣ Q 7 6        │W   E│         ♣ K J 9 4
                 │  S  │
                 └─────┘
                 ♠ Q 8 4
                 ♡ A K 4
                 ◇ A 8 6 4
                 ♣ 10 5 2
```

West	North	East	South
Schapiro	*Mathe*	*Reese*	*Bishop*
		Pass	1 ◇
Pass	1 ♡	Pass	1 NT
Pass	3 NT	All Pass	

As diamonds had been bid, West began with a low club, ducked in dummy. How would you expect the defence to go now?

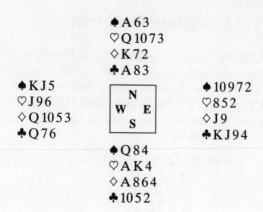

```
                    ♠A63
                    ♡Q1073
                    ◇K72
                    ♣A83
    ♠KJ5          ┌─────────┐      ♠10972
    ♡J96          │   N     │      ♡852
    ◇Q1053        │ W    E  │      ◇J9
    ♣Q76          │   S     │      ♣KJ94
                  └─────────┘
                    ♠Q84
                    ♡AK4
                    ◇A864
                    ♣1052
```

North-South played in three no-trumps after South had opened one diamond. West led a club to the king and . . .

But that's not right. Since he may need entries, and if South has the queen nothing will be lost, East put in the *jack* of clubs. Then he switched to the ten of spades and finally defeated the contract, though South can succeed at double dummy. At the other table North had no chance after a spade lead by East.

At this time there was none of the modern insistence on partnership. Most of the team played with at least three of the others at some point. Of course, they knew one another's game very well.

Teams nowadays go to war with an expert captain and a coach whose duty is to study the methods of opposing teams. Reg Corwen, the captain at Montreux and in America, was not a top-class player but he kept the team in a good mood with his straight-faced humour. Once, at Juan-les-Pins, his drive from the 11th tee nearly decapitated two players on an adjoining fairway. "Sorry I was a bit slow in calling," he said when he caught up with them. "I couldn't remember the French for Fore!"

Single Again

Back in 1954 the World Championship was a two-horse race, the Americans facing France, the European champions. The Frenchmen took up the option of strengthening their squad by forming a partnership between Jean Besse (Switzerland) and Karl Schneider (Austria). The Americans won, but Besse shone on this deal:

Love all; Dealer West.

♠ None
♡ A K Q 10 7 4 2
◇ K Q 8 7 3
♣ 4

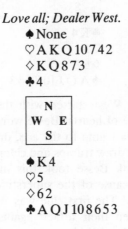

♠ K 4
♡ 5
◇ 6 2
♣ A Q J 10 8 6 5 3

West	North	East	South
Pass	2♡	Pass	3♣
Pass	3◇	Pass	5♣
Pass	6♣	All Pass	

Besse ended in six clubs and the American West led the ace of diamonds followed by the nine of hearts. How would you have played the slam?

This was the complete deal:

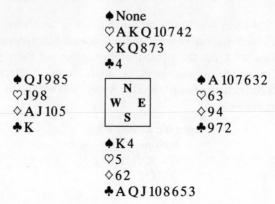

♠None
♡AKQ10742
♢KQ873
♣4

♠QJ985
♡J98
♢AJ105
♣K

N
W E
S

♠A107632
♡63
♢94
♣972

♠K4
♡5
♢62
♣AQJ108653

Against six clubs West started with the ace of diamonds, followed by the nine of hearts. Besse won the heart switch in dummy and played a trump to the ace, dropping West's bare king. He could then draw trumps and claim the contract.

Why do you think Besse took this inspired view of the trump suit? Not because of the superstition that the king of clubs is often single! The first clue was West's opening lead. Defenders who open their attack against a small slam by cashing the ace of a suit bid by the opponents usually have strong hopes for a second trick in their own hand. A second indication was West's play at trick two. If he did not hold the trump king himself he might well have played a spade, to remove dummy's singleton trump and thereby protect East's trump holding from a possible finesse.

Unavoidable Conclusion

Irish players are renowned for their forward bidding on slam hands. On this deal from a 1958 Irish trial Joe MacHale reached a slam that could politely be described as borderline.

Game all; Dealer South.

♠ K 10 9 8 4
♡ K 9 8 6 3
♢ 5 4
♣ A

```
    N
 W     E
    S
```

♠ A Q J 2
♡ A 7 2
♢ A J 2
♣ 10 5 4

West	North	East	South
			1 NT
Pass	2 ♣	2 ♢	2 ♠
Pass	4 NT	Pass	5 ♠
Pass	6 ♠	All Pass	

North's four no-trumps call was ambitious and not very well chosen, with two small in a side suit, particularly the suit bid by an opponent. A cue-bid of four clubs would be more sensible.

MacHale won East's queen of diamonds with the ace, crossed to the ace of clubs, and returned to the jack of spades to ruff a club. He continued with a second round of trumps and a club ruff. At this point East had followed to two spades and three clubs.

When a heart was led to the ace East contributed the queen. On the second round of hearts West played a small card. How should declarer continue?

This was the complete deal:

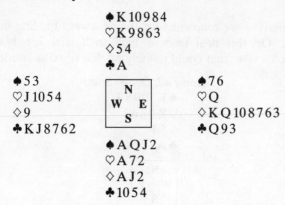

```
                    ♠ K 10 9 8 4
                    ♡ K 9 8 6 3
                    ◇ 5 4
                    ♣ A
    ♠ 5 3            ┌─────────┐        ♠ 7 6
    ♡ J 10 5 4       │   N     │        ♡ Q
    ◇ 9              │ W   E   │        ◇ K Q 10 8 7 6 3
    ♣ K J 8 7 6 2    │   S     │        ♣ Q 9 3
                    └─────────┘
                    ♠ A Q J 2
                    ♡ A 7 2
                    ◇ A J 2
                    ♣ 10 5 4
```

Declarer had to concede a heart trick to establish the two discards he needed. He could not afford to lose this trick to East, since East would obviously cash a diamond winner. Losing a heart trick to West would be fatal too, *unless West had no diamonds left.* Since declarer needed East to have started with seven diamonds, along with the five black-suit cards he had already shown, there was room for only one heart. MacHale therefore finessed the eight on the second round of hearts. When this hair-raising manoeuvre succeeded he had twelve tricks.

No doubt Joe was disappointed to learn that his side had lost on the board. In the other room West led the jack of hearts against the same contract. Declarer could now score five heart tricks and eventually ruff a diamond in the South hand. This gave him an overtrick!

Order of Play

The British ladies finished well down the list in the 1958 European Championships. This was one of their brighter moments, though, from their match against Sweden. It's a defensive position and you are sitting West.

Game all; Dealer East.

```
              ♠8
              ♡Q532
              ◇J943
              ♣8653
♠KQ4        ┌─────────┐
♡KJ84       │    N    │
◇Q76        │  W   E  │
♣J109       │    S    │
            └─────────┘
```

West	North	East	South
		Pass	2 NT[1]
Pass	3 NT	All pass	

[1] 20-22 points

You start with the jack of clubs and North displays her sub-minimal dummy. Partner produces the king of clubs and declarer wins with the ace. Ace, king and another diamond, your partner following all the way, puts you on lead with the diamond queen. What do you do now?

This was the complete deal:

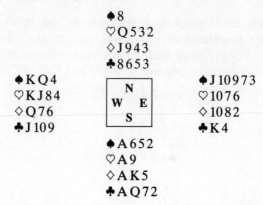

```
                    ♠8
                    ♡Q532
                    ◊J943
                    ♣8653
   ♠KQ4          ┌─────────┐      ♠J10973
   ♡KJ84         │    N    │      ♡1076
   ◊Q76          │ W     E │      ◊1082
   ♣J109         │    S    │      ♣K4
                 └─────────┘
                    ♠A652
                    ♡A9
                    ◊AK5
                    ♣AQ72
```

The play in three no-trumps starts with the jack of clubs to the king and ace, followed by ace, king and another diamond to West's queen. Did you find a switch to the king of spades now? So did the Swedish West (in her room defending only two no-trumps). East signalled heavily with the jack of spades and West continued with queen and another, declarer winning the third round. Now came queen and another club and West was endplayed, forced to open the hearts. Nine tricks resulted.

Marjorie Van Rees, the British West in the room where three no-trumps was bid, foresaw the endplay. When she won with the queen of diamonds she played the king and queen of spades, which South ducked. Now she made the smart return of the ten of clubs. It would do declarer no good to take this and play back a club because West would then have a safe exit in spades. Declarer therefore ducked the second round of clubs, hoping for a third round, which would give her time to set up the queen of hearts (the fourth round of clubs would provide an entry).

No such luck. Mrs Van Rees completed a polished performance by switching back to spades and game went one down.

Cutting the Ribbon

In 1960 two top French players, Bourchtoff and Delmouly, were invited to London to play in the Master Pairs. Whether this was adjudged a success when the Frenchmen won every session and finished a street ahead of the top English pairs of the time is not recorded.
Harrison-Gray pulled off a typical coup in the final session of the event.

Love all; Dealer East.

♠ K 8 7
♡ 9 5 2
♢ Q 9 4
♣ 10 7 5 3

```
      N
   W     E
      S
```

♠ A Q 6 2
♡ 8 7 6
♢ A J
♣ A J 8 4

West	North	East	South
Swimer	Flint	Preston	Gray
		Pass	1♣
1♡	Pass	1♠	1NT
2♡	2NT¹	Double	All Pass

¹ This may look bold, but South's one no-trump in such an exposed position suggested at least 17 points. Harrison-Gray's partners were not supposed to take into account the fact that he generally owed a point or two.

Gray won the spade lead with dummy's king and led a low club, East following with the six. With no re-entry to dummy, there was no point in trying the eight. Gray played the jack and this won the trick. How should declarer continue?

This was the complete deal:

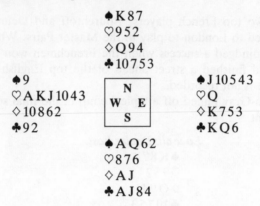

```
              ♠ K 8 7
              ♡ 9 5 2
              ◇ Q 9 4
              ♣ 10 7 5 3
♠ 9                          ♠ J 10 5 4 3
♡ A K J 10 4 3     N         ♡ Q
◇ 10 8 6 2     W     E       ◇ K 7 5 3
♣ 9 2              S         ♣ K Q 6
              ♠ A Q 6 2
              ♡ 8 7 6
              ◇ A J
              ♣ A J 8 4
```

Trying to reach partner's hand for a heart lead through declarer's supposed ♡Qxx, West led the nine of spades against two no-trumps doubled. Gray won with dummy's king and led a club to his jack, which held. Since West would have led a heart from a solid sequence, it was likely that East held a singleton queen or king in the suit. Aiming to cut the link between the defenders' hands, Gray's next move was a low heart from hand! Ralph Swimer, displaying less than his usual acumen, contributed the ten.

With West out of the play, Gray proceeded to set up the clubs and take finesses in both spades and diamonds. He ended with an overtrick.

At another table American ace Charles Goren, playing in an impromptu partnership with Boris Schapiro, landed in the same contract. He too found the brilliant play of a heart at trick three. The effect was somewhat marred when he repeated the manoeuvre on regaining the lead.

Sure Thing

An unexpected double of a slam contract, according to tradition, invites an unexpected lead: generally, not a trump and not the unbid suit, when this would be the natural choice. But when there has been a conventional opening bid, such as two clubs, does this count as an unbid suit? There seems to be no general agreement on this point. East-West had a calamitous misunderstanding on this deal from a Swiss tournament:

Game all; Dealer West.

♠ A Q J 10 9 8
♡ A K 10 7 6 3
♢ 9
♣ None

```
     N
  W     E
     S
```

♠ 7
♡ 4
♢ A K Q J 8 7 6 3
♣ K 3 2

North-South were playing two clubs Albarran — that is to say, with ace responses. The bidding went as follows:

West	North	East	South
Pass	2♣	Pass	3♢
Pass	3♠	Pass	4 NT
Pass	6♡	Pass	7 NT
Pass	Pass	Double	All Pass

Some misunderstanding about the response of six hearts, obviously. West led a low spade. Two questions arise:
(a) Should the declarer finesse? (b) If he does, and the finesse wins, how should he continue?

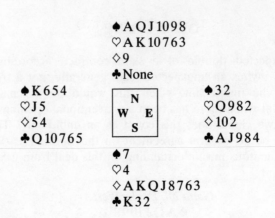

♠AQJ1098
♡AK10763
◇9
♣None

♠K654 ♠32
♡J5 ♡Q982
◇54 ◇102
♣Q10765 ♣AJ984

♠7
♡4
◇AKQJ8763
♣K32

South is playing in seven no-trumps, doubled by East, and West leads a low spade. The first question was, should he finesse? Certainly, because there is no reason to expect a singleton king in East's hand, and if the finesse were wrong there would be only a remote chance for thirteen tricks (a possible squeeze if East held ace of clubs and four low hearts).

The second question was, how should South continue after a spade finesse at trick one? Answer: he should lay down his cards, announcing that he will cash the ace of spades, then run all the diamonds, with a sure double squeeze, West being marked with the king of spades and East with the ace of clubs.

Handsome Finish

Back in 1963 a heavy international contingent attended the first Lebanese Festival of Bridge. In the teams final Joe Tarlo played brilliantly on this deal:

Game all; Dealer South.

♠Q984
♡76
◇AK54
♣K42

```
    N
 W    E
    S
```

♠K6
♡AJ9852
◇Q98
♣97

West led the jack of spades against Tarlo's contract of four hearts. Declarer won with the king and returned another spade to the eight and ace. East played a club to West's ace and a second club was taken by dummy's king. Declarer had already lost to the black aces, so he had to pick up the trumps for one loser. He ran the seven of hearts and this card held, West producing the four. How would you proceed at this point?

This was the complete deal:

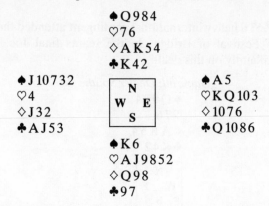

```
                    ♠Q984
                    ♡76
                    ◇AK54
                    ♣K42
♠J10732                              ♠A5
♡4              N                    ♡KQ103
◇J32        W       E                ◇1076
♣AJ53              S                 ♣Q1086
                    ♠K6
                    ♡AJ9852
                    ◇Q98
                    ♣97
```

The play in four hearts started: jack of spades to the king, spade to the eight and ace, club to West's ace, and a club to dummy's king. Next came seven of hearts from dummy. It was difficult for East to see that he should split his equals and he played the three. Declarer ran the seven, which held the trick.

Tarlo ruffed a club in hand, crossed to the king of diamonds, and led the nine of spades. East discarded a diamond and declarer ruffed once more, reducing his trumps to the same length as that of East. A diamond to the ace left this position:

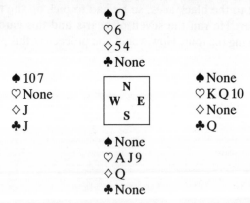

```
                    ♠Q
                    ♡6
                    ◇54
                    ♣None
♠107                                 ♠None
♡None           N                    ♡KQ10
◇J          W       E                ◇None
♣J                 S                 ♣Q
                    ♠None
                    ♡AJ9
                    ◇Q
                    ♣None
```

Declarer led the queen of spades and East ruffed with the king. Tarlo underruffed with the nine. He could then ruff East's queen of clubs return in the dummy and lead a plain card towards his ace-jack of hearts. Ten tricks made.

Had East split his honours on the first round of trumps, declarer would have had one too few entries to dummy to achieve a similar end position.

Tooth and Nail

This deal from the 1963 world championship between Italy and the USA caused much wonder in its day. If Garozzo's play seems a little less remarkable now, this may be because standards have improved all round. Not that *many* players would do the same as he did.

Game all; Dealer West.

```
              ♠74
              ♡43
              ◇Q8
              ♣K1098642
 ♠QJ105         N         ♠2
 ♡Q1095    W        E     ♡A8762
 ◇107           S         ◇A532
 ♣QJ5                     ♣A73
              ♠AK9863
              ♡KJ
              ◇KJ964
              ♣None
```

West	North	East	South
Forquet	*Schenken*	*Garozzo*	*Nail*
Pass	Pass	1♡	Double[1]
2♡	3♣	Pass	3♠
Pass	4♣	Pass	4◇
Pass	4♠	Pass	Pass
Double	All Pass		

[1] Not everyone's choice. Why not one spade and see how things develop?

West led a heart to the ace and a spade was returned. South won and played a diamond to the queen. How will the play go now, do you think?

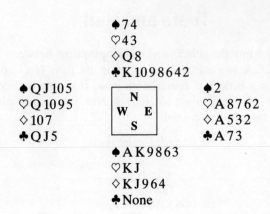

♠ 74
♡ 43
◇ Q 8
♣ K 10 9 8 6 4 2

♠ Q J 10 5   ♠ 2
♡ Q 10 9 5   ♡ A 8 7 6 2
◇ 10 7   ◇ A 5 3 2
♣ Q J 5   ♣ A 7 3

♠ A K 9 8 6 3
♡ K J
◇ K J 9 6 4
♣ None

It's quite simple. When South, in four spades doubled, led a diamond to the queen, East played low; and when a diamond was returned, East again played low. Thinking now that West might hold ◇ A x and East ◇ 10 x x x, Bobby Nail put in the nine and so went two down. It cost seven match points since at the other table the same contract was only one down.

Ducking the diamond twice was not in the least risky; South had bid diamonds, and one round of trumps had already been played, so East was sure to make the ace whatever happened on the second round of the suit. It's awful to recall, but one writer headed his column, "A Nail-biting Affair".

False Assumption

South is dealer on the two hands below. How do you think the bidding should go?

♠ Q 8
♡ 10 6 3
◇ A Q J 9 6
♣ A Q 4

♠ A K 9 6
♡ J 9 2
◇ 4
♣ K J 9 8 3

This would be a fair auction:

West	North	East	South
			1♣
Pass	1◇	Pass	1♠
Pass	2♡	Pass	2 NT
Pass	3 NT	All Pass	

Although South has no secure heart stop, two no-trumps is the most descriptive call on the third round.

When the deal arose in the 1964 US Olympic Trials, B.J. Becker and his partner had a less impressive sequence:

West	North	East	South
			1♣
Pass	1◇	Pass	1♠
Pass	3♣[1]	Pass	4♣[2]
Pass	4♠[3]	Pass	6♣[4]

[1] Forcing.
[2] Intended as natural but read as Gerber.
[3] Intended to show two aces, but read as a partial spade fit.
[4] South deduces that his partner must be short in hearts!

How would you play this contract when West leads ace, king and queen of hearts? No, we'll give you a chance; West leads the two of diamonds.

This was the full deal:

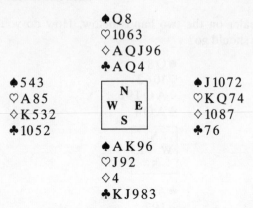

```
                    ♠Q8
                    ♡1063
                    ◇AQJ96
                    ♣AQ4
   ♠543                          ♠J1072
   ♡A85          ┌─────────┐    ♡KQ74
   ◇K532         │   N     │    ◇1087
   ♣1052         │ W   E   │    ♣76
                 │   S     │
                 └─────────┘
                    ♠AK96
                    ♡J92
                    ◇4
                    ♣KJ983
```

Playing in six clubs, Becker called for dummy's queen on the diamond lead. He then cashed the ace, discarding a heart, and ruffed a diamond. A trump to the ace was followed by a second diamond ruff and the king and queen of trumps.

Dummy's last diamond was led in this end position:

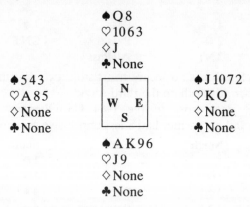

```
                    ♠Q8
                    ♡1063
                    ◇J
                    ♣None
   ♠543                          ♠J1072
   ♡A85          ┌─────────┐    ♡KQ
   ◇None         │   N     │    ◇None
   ♣None         │ W   E   │    ♣None
                 │   S     │
                 └─────────┘
                    ♠AK96
                    ♡J9
                    ◇None
                    ♣None
```

The last diamond collected the queen, nine and five of hearts. It was clear that East was down to four spades and a bare heart honour. Becker cashed the queen of spades and led the eight, intending to run it. East in fact split his honours and declarer won with the ace.

Now came the jack of hearts from the South hand. If West went up with the ace, he would have to give the last two tricks to dummy's ♡106. In fact he played low; East won with the king and had to lead from ♠J7 into declarer's ♠K9.

Perhaps Becker and his partner *did* know what they were doing in the bidding!

Young Pretenders

When Garozzo and Belladonnna were at the height of their fame in the 1960s they accepted a challenge at rubber bridge from two young players. (One of them was Arturo Franco, who later became an outstanding member of Italian teams.) On the following deal Garozzo found a line of play that might not occur to you even with a sight of all the hands.

Game all; Dealer North.

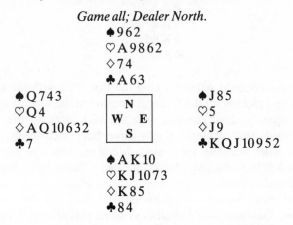

```
              ♠962
              ♡A9862
              ◇74
              ♣A63
♠Q743                        ♠J85
♡Q4          N               ♡5
◇AQ10632   W   E             ◇J9
♣7             S             ♣KQJ10952
              ♠AK10
              ♡KJ1073
              ◇K85
              ♣84
```

West	North	East	South
	Pass	3♣	3♡[1]
Pass	4♡	All Pass	

[1] Most players would count their points and double. Benito likes to play the hand, even when his partner is Belladonna.

West led his singleton club, won by the ace. There seem to be four losers. What do you suppose was Garozzo's line of play?

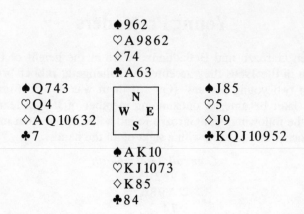

```
              ♠962
              ♡A9862
              ◇74
              ♣A63
♠Q743         ┌─────────┐      ♠J85
♡Q4           │    N    │      ♡5
◇AQ10632      │ W     E │      ◇J9
♣7            │    S    │      ♣KQJ10952
              └─────────┘
              ♠AK10
              ♡KJ1073
              ◇K85
              ♣84
```

Simple enough! After winning the first trick with the ace of clubs and picking up the trumps, Benito led the nine of spades from dummy. East covered with the jack, making the point afterwards that declarer might have held such as ♠ K 10 x. South won with the king, then followed with ace and ten, which left West on play, forced to lead a diamond or concede a ruff-and-discard.

Had East been inspired enough to hold off the jack of spades, Garozzo would doubtless have played ace, king and another spade, hoping to find West with both spade honours (or any five spades). West would then have defeated the contract by letting his partner take the ten of spades.

Hidden Strength

In the semi-finals of the 1967 Vanderbilt, Walsh beat Kaplan by a fair margin and went on to beat Stayman in the final. Kaplan had a bright moment on this deal, though.

Game all; Dealer North.

♠ 9 5 3
♡ 10 9 4 2
◇ K 9 6 3
♣ 7 4

```
    N
W       E
    S
```

♠ K J 7 2
♡ A K 8 6 3
◇ A 10 4
♣ A

West	North	East	South
Hallee	*Kay*	*Soloway*	*Kaplan*
	Pass	Pass	1♡
Pass	1NT[1]	Pass	2♠[2]
Pass	3♡	Pass	4♡
All Pass			

[1] Aiming to shut out the opponents . . .
[2] . . . but failing to shut out his partner.

West led a low club to East's queen and declarer's ace. It seemed to Kaplan that the very least he would need would be a 2-2 trump break, but when he cashed ace and king of hearts East discarded a high club on the second round. A heart was played to West's queen and West exited safely with a club to East's king, ruffed by declarer.

What should declarer do now?

This was the full deal:

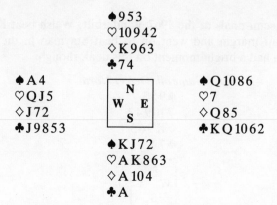

♠953
♡10942
◇K963
♣74

♠A4
♡QJ5
◇J72
♣J9853

N
W E
S

♠Q1086
♡7
◇Q85
♣KQ10062

♠KJ72
♡AK863
◇A104
♣A

The early play in four hearts went: club to the queen and ace; ace, king and another heart to West's queen; club exit ruffed. Kaplan reckoned that it was too much to hope for queen-jack doubleton in diamonds. A better chance was to find West with a doubleton spade ace, forcing him to open the diamonds.

At trick six declarer led a spade to the nine and ten. When the six of spades was returned Kaplan played the seven! West's ace appeared, as if by magic, and was followed smartly by the jack of diamonds. It seemed to Edgar that if West's diamonds had been headed by the ◇QJ he might have chosen a diamond opening lead rather than a club. He therefore called for dummy's king of diamonds and finessed the ten on the way back. Ten tricks made.

Part 3

Not Quite So Well Played

Or, in some cases, not quite so well bid.

Small Oversight

The North-South hands on this deal from the 1988 Olympiad contained 33 points between them, usually enough for six no-trumps, but players in three no-trumps had to fight for their ninth trick and there were many casualties at higher levels.

North-South game; Dealer West.

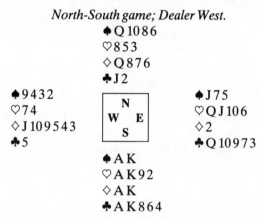

```
              ♠ Q 10 8 6
              ♡ 8 5 3
              ◇ Q 8 7 6
              ♣ J 2
♠ 9 4 3 2                      ♠ J 7 5
♡ 7 4          N               ♡ Q J 10 6
◇ J 10 9 5 4 3  W   E          ◇ 2
♣ 5              S             ♣ Q 10 9 7 3
              ♠ A K
              ♡ A K 9 2
              ◇ A K
              ♣ A K 8 6 4
```

If you picked up the South hand, even in fourth position, you might expect a free run, but things are not like that in the modern world. In the match between Canada and New Zealand this was the bidding with Canada North-South:

West	North	East	South
Crombie	*Murray*	*Reid*	*Kehela*
1♠	Pass	3♣	Double
Pass	3♠	Pass	3 NT
All Pass			

West's one spade was what is riskily called a 'fert' (short for fertiliser), showing 0-8 or a balanced nine points. East's three clubs was designed to maintain the pre-empt.

West led his singleton club against three no-trumps — can you believe it? — and it wasn't difficult for South to develop his ninth trick.

At the other table the Canadian West opened three diamonds and Molson, East, responded three hearts (a sort of semi-psychic: let opponents think it's a non-existent suit). South forced his way to six no-trumps, more or less on his own.

What do you think happened in this contract?

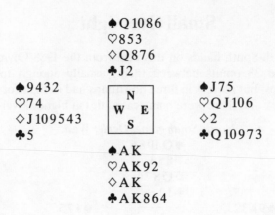

♠Q1086
♥853
♦Q876
♣J2

♠9432 ♠J75
♥74 ♥QJ106
♦J109543 ♦2
♣5 ♣Q10973

♠AK
♥AK92
♦AK
♣AK864

Against six no-trumps, West led a heart (again a dreadful choice) to the ten and ace. South cashed the top spades and diamonds, then led a club to the jack and queen.

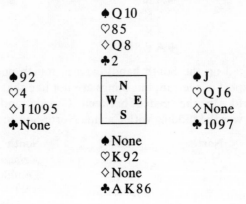

♠Q10
♥85
♦Q8
♣2

♠92 ♠J
♥4 ♥QJ6
♦J1095 ♦None
♣None ♣1097

♠None
♥K92
♦None
♣AK86

Obviously a heart or club from East at this point would lead to two down, but Molson, unfortunately for his team, had missed his partner's delicate high-low in spades. Thinking that South still had a spade he returned the jack now, with the idea of forcing the declarer to a problematical discard on the fourth spade. A squeeze followed, for twelve tricks.

East, it is said, was so shaken that he left the table for several minutes before he felt able to resume play. The mystery is that he ever came back.

Not Intending to Deceive

This was another battle of the major suits. Italy and the USA, the old adversaries, were facing each other in the 1975 World Championships.

East-West game; Dealer West.

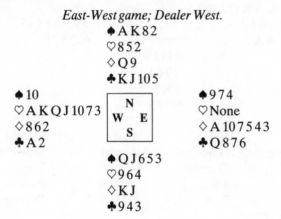

♠ A K 8 2
♡ 8 5 2
◇ Q 9
♣ K J 10 5

♠ 10
♡ A K Q J 10 7 3
◇ 8 6 2
♣ A 2

♠ 9 7 4
♡ None
◇ A 10 7 5 4 3
♣ Q 8 7 6

♠ Q J 6 5 3
♡ 9 6 4
◇ K J
♣ 9 4 3

West	North	East	South
Franco	*Wolff*	*Pittala*	*Hamman*
1♡	Double	2◇	2♠
4♡	4♠	Double	All Pass

The Italians dropped a trick in defence. Franco cashed three rounds of hearts and switched to a diamond. East won with the ace and returned a diamond to declarer's king. After drawing trumps, declarer led a club towards dummy and Franco (who had a complete count on the hand) unwisely ducked. Hamman called for dummy's king and a second round of clubs endplayed West. Only 500 to East-West.

It seemed that the Americans would gain heavily when their West player, Billy Eisenberg, arrived in five hearts doubled. Can you imagine how this contract went down?

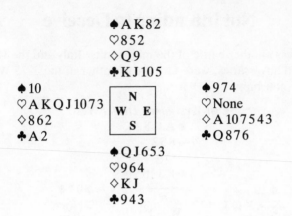

```
                    ♠ A K 8 2
                    ♡ 8 5 2
                    ◇ Q 9
                    ♣ K J 10 5
    ♠ 10                              ♠ 9 7 4
    ♡ A K Q J 10 7 3      N          ♡ None
    ◇ 8 6 2           W     E        ◇ A 10 7 5 4 3
    ♣ A 2                 S          ♣ Q 8 7 6
                    ♠ Q J 6 5 3
                    ♡ 9 6 4
                    ◇ K J
                    ♣ 9 4 3
```

West	North	East	South
Eisenberg	*Garozzo*	*Kantar*	*Belladonna*
1♡	Double	2◇	2♠
4♡	4♠	Double	Pass
5♡	Pass	Pass	Double
All Pass			

Again West opens one heart! In the opinion of the old-
fashioned authors it is ridiculous not to open four hearts (or
four clubs, if that shows a strong four heart opening). One
time in ten you may miss a slam; five times in ten you will have
the better of a competitive deal.

Garozzo led the king of spades and at trick two switched to
a diamond, the *nine*! When declarer played low from dummy,
South won with the king and led the four of clubs. Declarer
put up the ace of clubs and drew trumps.

Eleven tricks were now his if the diamonds were 2–2.
Eisenberg, distracted by North's nine of diamonds switch,
could not believe this was so. He therefore played safely for
one down (in five, remember) by leading a club towards the
queen, establishing a diamond discard. A grateful Garozzo
hopped up with the king to put the contract one down.

Eisenberg's reasoning does not perhaps survive close
inspection. North would scarcely have risked a switch from
◇ Q J 9; and if the nine were a singleton, surely South would
have won with the jack of diamonds and returned the king,
removing the entry to dummy.

'I Want You All to Know'

It is strange how, even at international level, players on the defending side persist in making quite pointless doubles when an opponent names a suit where they have length or strength. Look at this example from the match between Pakistan and Indonesia in the Stockholm Olympiad.

Love all; Dealer East.

```
              ♠ J 10 4 3
              ♡ J 3 2
              ◇ Q J 7 5 4 2
              ♣ None
♠ Q 8 5          ┌─────────┐      ♠ 9 7 6
♡ 9 6 4          │   N     │      ♡ 7 5
◇ 8 3            │ W   E   │      ◇ A K 10 9 6
♣ K 10 8 5 2     │   S     │      ♣ J 6 3
                 └─────────┘
              ♠ A K 2
              ♡ A K Q 10 8
              ◇ None
              ♣ A Q 9 7 4
```

West	North	East	South
Munawar	*Salim*	*Jasin*	*Mahmood*
		Pass	2♣
Pass	2◇	Double¹	2♡
Pass	3◇²	Pass	4♣
Double³	5♣⁴	Pass	6♡
All Pass			

¹ Here it begins. 'I wanted to show you a lead', they say.
² Just showing his distribution, apparently; but the bid may have conveyed support for hearts.
³ What good will this do? You might as well show your cards to the opponents.
⁴ North is able to make a cue-bid indicating short clubs, probably a void.

Armed with the information he had been given, how do you suppose Zia played six hearts? West led a diamond.

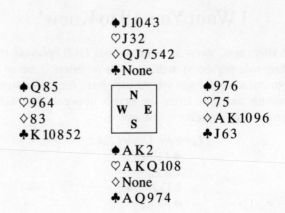

```
                    ♠ J1043
                    ♡ J32
                    ◇ QJ7542
                    ♣ None
  ♠ Q85            N            ♠ 976
  ♡ 964        W       E        ♡ 75
  ◇ 83             S            ◇ AK1096
  ♣ K10852                      ♣ J63
                    ♠ AK2
                    ♡ AKQ108
                    ◇ None
                    ♣ AQ974
```

Playing in six hearts after East had doubled diamonds and West had doubled clubs, Zia played a combined crossruff and throw-in: he ruffed three clubs in dummy, using top spades for entry, drew trumps, and threw West in on the third round of spades, forcing a lead into ♣AQ. Other declarers went one or two down in six hearts.

Another example of this type of folly occurred in the World Top Tournament at the Hague:

Game all, Dealer West.

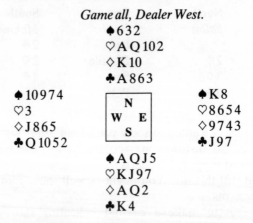

```
                    ♠ 632
                    ♡ AQ102
                    ◇ K10
                    ♣ A863
  ♠ 10974          N            ♠ K8
  ♡ 3          W       E        ♡ 8654
  ◇ J865           S            ◇ 9743
  ♣ Q1052                       ♣ J97
                    ♠ AQJ5
                    ♡ KJ97
                    ◇ AQ2
                    ♣ K4
```

At one point in the auction between Greece and the USA, North responded five spades to South's four no-trumps. Goldman, East, doubled; not so much a Greek gift as a gift to the Greeks. South promptly went to seven hearts, for a gain of 11 IMPs.

Is the Score Right?

Would you fancy your chances in six diamonds on the deal below? You never can tell, even at world championship level. Mind you, you will have to play it cleverly and encounter imperfect defence.

Game all; Dealer East.

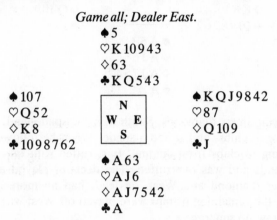

```
                    ♠5
                    ♡K10943
                    ◇63
                    ♣KQ543
        ♠107                      ♠KQJ9842
        ♡Q52          N           ♡87
        ◇K8        W   E          ◇Q109
        ♣1098762      S           ♣J
                    ♠A63
                    ♡AJ6
                    ◇AJ7542
                    ♣A
```

This was the bidding in a match between Italy and Brazil:

West	North	East	South
Chagas	*Franco*	*Branco*	*De Falco*
		3♠	4◇
Pass	5◇	Pass	6◇
All Pass			

West led the ten of spades and the report from the closed room was that the contract had been made. The Vugraph commentators had to send a messenger to discover how it had been done. What was the answer?

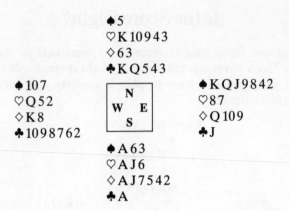

Playing in six diamonds, South won the spade lead, cashed the ace of clubs, and ruffed a spade. When he followed with the king of clubs from dummy, East ruffed with the nine of diamonds and was overruffed. The declarer played ace and another diamond and West, on lead, had no more spades. When the remaining trumps were played off West was caught in a show-up squeeze:

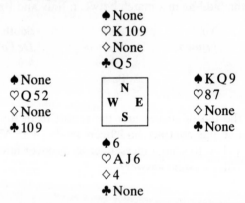

East's ruff with the nine of diamonds was an error. What was the declarer trying to do, leading the king of clubs before drawing trumps?

Meanwhile, the great Chagas, hero of so many brilliancies, missed one when he failed to drop the king of diamonds under the ace! East could then have won the second round of trumps and cashed a spade trick.

The French Connection

The teams event at the Juan-Les-Pins tournament is a special sort of affair, in which you meet every other team in short matches over three days. The highly accomplished team of Albarran and Meredith, Stayman and Solomon, had a strange experience on the following deal against relatively unknown opposition.

East-West game; Dealer East.

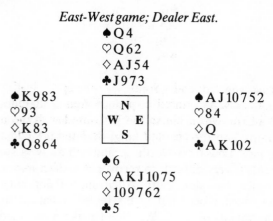

```
              ♠Q4
              ♡Q62
              ◇AJ54
              ♣J973
   ♠K983              ♠AJ10752
   ♡93         N       ♡84
   ◇K83      W   E     ◇Q
   ♣Q864       S       ♣AK102
              ♠6
              ♡AKJ1075
              ◇109762
              ♣5
```

West	North	East	South
Meredith		*Albarran*	
		1♠	2♡
2♠	3♡	4♠	5♡
Double	All Pass		

After a spade lead to the ace, East tried to cash two rounds of clubs. Declarer ruffed the second round, drew trumps, and advanced the ten of diamonds. Now 'Plum' Meredith made one of his very rare mistakes. He covered with the king of diamonds! 650 to the French pair.

At the other table the bidding was:

West	North	East	South
	Stayman		*Solomon*
		1♠	2♡
2♠	3♡	4♠	5♡
Pass	Pass	5♠	Pass
Pass	Double	All Pass	

What do you think happened this time?

49

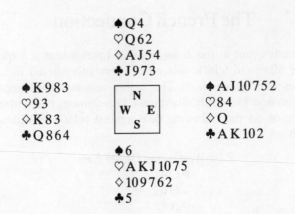

♠ Q 4
♥ Q 6 2
♦ A J 5 4
♣ J 9 7 3

♠ K 9 8 3   ♠ A J 10 7 5 2
♥ 9 3   ♥ 8 4
♦ K 8 3   ♦ Q
♣ Q 8 6 4   ♣ A K 10 2

♠ 6
♥ A K J 10 7 5
♦ 10 9 7 6 2
♣ 5

You have guessed, of course.

Solomon cashed two hearts against five spades doubled, then led a club, which ran to the jack and ace. The declarer drew trumps with the ace and king, then led a low diamond from dummy. Low from North... and 850 away, a swing of 1500, 19 IMPs, *very* difficult to recover in a short match.

The French champion, Pierre Albarran, had not said a word when the disaster occurred at his table. 'What an unlucky board,' he remarked now. 'We didn't make a diamond trick at either table.'

The Boss Suit

Early reports of this deal from a world championship match between Canada and the USA made much of the bidding but said nothing about the play, which was really rather interesting.

East-West game; Dealer West.

```
              ♠ None
              ♡ K976
              ◇ AQ953
              ♣ K986
♠ Q108                          ♠ AKJ653
♡ 8543         N                ♡ 2
◇ 82         W   E              ◇ K64
♣ QJ42         S                ♣ A105
              ♠ 9742
              ♡ AQJ10
              ◇ J107
              ♣ 73
```

West	North	East	South
Forbes	*Robinson*	*Howell*	*Jordan*
Pass	1◇	2♠	Pass
Pass	Double	Pass	4♡
Pass	Pass	Double	All Pass

East-West missed an easy game their way — there are eleven tricks in spades after a diamond lead. East was strong for the jump overcall; West might have raised.

West led a spade against four hearts and dummy ruffed. Declarer played a trump to the queen, then ran the jack of diamonds. East won and played another spade. Now South had an easy ten tricks.

Two small errors were made in the play. Can you say what they were?

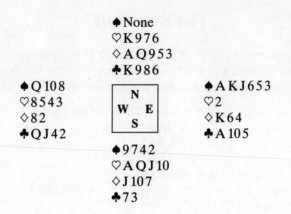

```
                     ♠ None
                     ♡ K976
                     ◇ A Q 9 5 3
                     ♣ K 9 8 6
      ♠ Q 108                      ♠ A K J 6 5 3
      ♡ 8543          N             ♡ 2
      ◇ 82        W       E         ◇ K 6 4
      ♣ Q J 4 2        S            ♣ A 105
                     ♠ 9742
                     ♡ A Q J 10
                     ◇ J 107
                     ♣ 7 3
```

We said there were two mistakes in the play:

(1) South wants to drive out the king of diamonds. He should lead the ten of diamonds to the queen, making it much more difficult for East to hold off.

(2) As the play went, East should have held up the king of diamonds. It is impossible, then, for South to make ten tricks.

This was the bidding at the other table:

West	North	East	South
Mitchell	*Kehela*	*Stayman*	*Murray*
Pass	1◇	1♠ [1]	2◇ [2]
Pass	3◇	3♠	All Pass

[1] You hold the boss suit, you can double. Partner bids hearts, you bid spades, no harm done.

[2] Nowadays a negative double would be preferred, bringing the heart fit to light.

The American pair, having made eleven tricks, must have been relieved to find they had gained 13 IMPs on the board.

At Sixes and Sevens

One of the recurring problems in this game is whether you should lead an ace against a small slam. Sometimes it is essential to establish a trick in another suit before your ace is knocked out. On other occasions it is a question of 'now or never'.

On this deal from an ancient piece of border warfare between Mexico and the USA the Mexican defender make the right first move by laying down the ace of a side suit. There was still a problem — what to do next.

Love all; Dealer North.

♠ None
♡ K Q J 9 8
♢ J
♣ K Q J 8 7 4 2

♠ Q J 10 9 4 2
♡ 6 5 2
♢ 6 4
♣ A 5

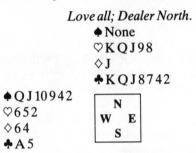

West	North	East	South
Weil	*Jordan*	*Fischer*	*Robinson*
	1♣	Pass	1♢
2♠	3♡	Pass	4♢
Pass	4♡	Pass	4♠
Pass	5♣	Pass	6♢
All Pass			

Despite his strong distribution, it was incautious of North to bid three hearts over West's two spades. Three clubs is sounder; he can follow with three hearts over the likely three diamonds.

West led the ace of clubs, on which East played the three and declarer the six. What should West do now, do you think?

The full deal was:

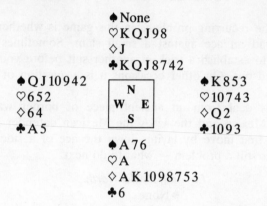

```
              ♠ None
              ♡ K Q J 9 8
              ◇ J
              ♣ K Q J 8 7 4 2
♠ Q J 10 9 4 2        ┌─────┐        ♠ K 8 5 3
♡ 6 5 2               │  N  │        ♡ 10 7 4 3
◇ 6 4            W    │     │    E   ◇ Q 2
♣ A 5                 │  S  │        ♣ 10 9 3
                      └─────┘
              ♠ A 7 6
              ♡ A
              ◇ A K 10 9 8 7 5 3
              ♣ 6
```

Correctly reading the six of clubs as a singleton, West led a heart at trick two, enabling South to dispose of his two losers. He said afterwards that he placed the declarer with something like:

♠ A K x   ♡ x   ◇ A K Q x x x x x   ♣ x.

With a hand of this type South would surely have launched into a Blackwood four no-trumps.

The winning play at trick two (also if South had held the hand of which West was afear'd) is a trump. Might kill partner's possible ◇ Q x x, did you say? Not really, for two reasons: if South held seven diamonds to the A K 10 he would cross to dummy for a finesse if dummy had an entry; and if dummy had no entry there would surely be a loser in spades.

In the other room the Mexican North-South pair was even more ambitious, attempting seven clubs. The American West ventured to double this and Mexico lost another 100. It was 14 IMPs to the USA.

Floor Show

Appointed to report on the play in a junior trial, one of the present authors saw two game contracts put on the floor. Each involved the management of a two-suiter. The first should perhaps have been within the reach of a budding international:

North-South game; Dealer South.

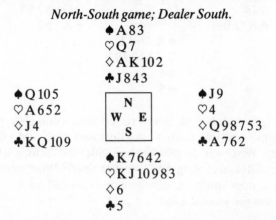

North hand:
♠A83
♡Q7
◇AK102
♣J843

West hand:
♠Q105
♡A652
◇J4
♣KQ109

East hand:
♠J9
♡4
◇Q98753
♣A762

South hand:
♠K7642
♡KJ10983
◇6
♣5

South passed as dealer, earning a good mark in the kibitzer's book. He was able to enter later and became declarer in four hearts. He ruffed the second club and played on trumps. Forced to ruff again, he had to expend all his trumps to draw those of West and so ran out of steam, losing the last two tricks.

What was wrong with that line of play?

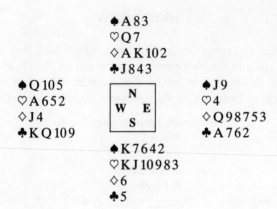

♠ A 83
♥ Q 7
♦ A K 10 2
♣ J 8 4 3

♠ Q 10 5   ♠ J 9
♥ A 6 5 2   ♥ 4
♦ J 4   ♦ Q 9 8 7 5 3
♣ K Q 10 9   ♣ A 7 6 2

♠ K 7 6 4 2
♥ K J 10 9 8 3
♦ 6
♣ 5

Playing in four hearts, South ruffed the second club, played on trumps, and lost control. As on many shaky two-suiters, the game here was to play on the side suit before drawing trumps. After ace, king and another spade West may force again, but now South can continue on cross-ruff lines.

This was the second hand:

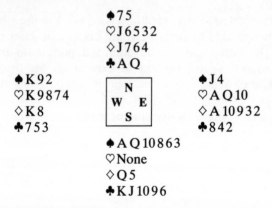

♠ 7 5
♥ J 6 5 3 2
♦ J 7 6 4
♣ A Q

♠ K 9 2   ♠ J 4
♥ K 9 8 7 4   ♥ A Q 10
♦ K 8   ♦ A 10 9 3 2
♣ 7 5 3   ♣ 8 4 2

♠ A Q 10 8 6 3
♥ None
♦ Q 5
♣ K J 10 9 6

Playing in four spades, South ruffed the heart lead, crossed to the ace of clubs, and finessed the ten of spades, losing to the king. After consulting his ancestors West switched to the king of diamonds and obtained a trump promotion on the third round.

Not so easy to see in time that South should discard a diamond on the opening lead instead of ruffing.

Dubious Offer

In an American Life Masters event North-South held:

♠KQJ53
♡105
◇754
♣842

```
    ┌─────┐
    │  N  │
    │W   E│
    │  S  │
    └─────┘
```

♠A
♡AKQ9763
◇AK3
♣A10

Following a sequence which need not be committed to posterity, Kantar and Lawrence arrived at seven no-trumps. They were doing well in the tournament and so were their opponents (Weinstein and Stewart). West led the queen of diamonds.

Playing in seven no-trumps at this critical moment, what do you consider is the most sensible line to follow?

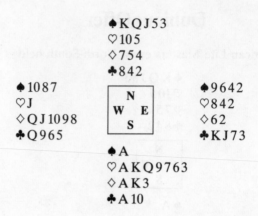

```
                    ♠KQJ53
                    ♡105
                    ◇754
                    ♣842
    ♠1087            N           ♠9642
    ♡J          W       E        ♡842
    ◇QJ1098          S           ◇62
    ♣Q965                        ♣KJ73
                    ♠A
                    ♡AKQ9763
                    ◇AK3
                    ♣A10
```

South was in seven no-trumps and West led the queen of diamonds. Simple folk would lay down the ace of hearts, hoping desperately for a singleton jack, about a 12% chance. But Lawrence cashed the ace of spades and then advanced the nine of hearts, losing to the singleton jack.

Lawrence's play was hailed in the American press as the unluckiest venture since the first Bird-man took to the air. He was aiming to finish level with players in six hearts, who would probably go one down after a diamond lead.

Let's look at that more closely. First, players in a small slam might follow the same line and make the contract on occasions when Lawrence would go one down. Second, nothing would be gained if East held ♡Jx or ♡Jxx, because it would be easy for him to duck. West probably would take the jack rather than risk the calamity that would occur if declarer decided to overtake with dummy's ten (as he might if West had given the matter the very faintest thought).

All things considered, it is probably wise to lay down the ace of hearts. (The opponents who had such good fortune on this deal won the event.)

Part 4

Penalty Points

A few hands where large penalties occurred,
for reasons not at all easy to foresee.

A Girl's Best Friend

The 1952 World Championship match was contested between Sweden and the USA, the Americans eventually winning by 8250 aggregate over 256 boards. The Swedes did well on this board, though. Try it first as an opening lead problem. At game all the bidding goes:

West	North	East	South
			1♣
Pass	1♠	Pass	2♠
Pass	3◇	Pass	3NT
All Pass			

Wohlin, sitting West for Sweden, had to lead from these cards:

♠843
♡AJ85
◇Q83
♣K86

Hearts, the unbid suit, is one possibility. South is likely to be short in diamonds, though; perhaps that would be a better attack. Which card would you choose?

This was the complete deal:

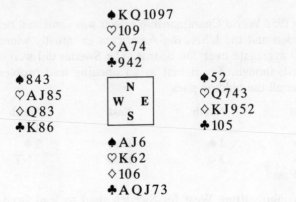

```
                    ♠ K Q 10 9 7
                    ♡ 10 9
                    ◇ A 7 4
                    ♣ 9 4 2
    ♠ 8 4 3                          ♠ 5 2
    ♡ A J 8 5         N              ♡ Q 7 4 3
    ◇ Q 8 3      W         E         ◇ K J 9 5 2
    ♣ K 8 6          S              ♣ 10 5
                    ♠ A J 6
                    ♡ K 6 2
                    ◇ 10 6
                    ♣ A Q J 7 3
```

If you lead a heart against three no-trumps declarer will come to nine tricks; the club finesse loses but you will then take only one club and three hearts.

The queen of diamonds would have been a good card in some circumstances (South a singleton jack or ten), but Wohlin's eight of diamonds was a good choice too. Declarer rose with the ace and finessed in clubs. The defenders now had a field day. West played the queen of diamonds, East overtaking and cashing out the suit. East then led the *queen* of hearts and the defenders took four more tricks in that suit. That was five down for a penalty of 500.

In the other room Kock, the Swedish North, played in four spades. A heart lead followed by a diamond switch would have defeated this, but the US East led the five of diamonds. Since he could not allow East to gain the lead later, Kock made the essential move of ducking the queen of diamonds at trick one. He won the diamond continuation and ruffed a diamond high. He then returned to hand with a trump and finessed the queen of clubs. West allowed this to win but declarer could now draw trumps and repeat the club finesse into the safe hand. A further 620 to the Swedes.

Why Wait?

Giorgio Belladonna was once asked what was the best counter to the Precision one club opening that he favoured at the time. "Bid Three Spades!" he suggested.

Overcalling a strong club is not without risk, though. Belladonna and Garozzo themselves applied the axe on this deal from a match between the Precision team and Ireland.

Game all; Dealer East.

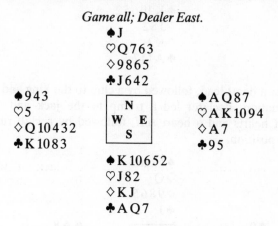

```
                    ♠ J
                    ♡ Q 7 6 3
                    ◇ 9 8 6 5
                    ♣ J 6 4 2
     ♠ 9 4 3                        ♠ A Q 8 7
     ♡ 5          ┌─────────┐       ♡ A K 10 9 4
     ◇ Q 10 4 3 2 │ N       │       ◇ A 7
     ♣ K 10 8 3   │ W     E │       ♣ 9 5
                  │   S     │
                  └─────────┘
                    ♠ K 10 6 5 2
                    ♡ J 8 2
                    ◇ K J
                    ♣ A Q 7
```

West	North	East	South
Garozzo		*Belladonna*	
		1♣	Pass
1◇	Pass	1♡	1♠
Double	All Pass		

West's double was negative, indicating values in the two unbid suits and little support for hearts. East was happy to convert it into a penalty double. Note that it was poor tactics for South to enter the auction on the second round rather than the first. If the bidding had started 1♣—1♠—Double, East would hardly be in a position to leave it, since his partner might hold heart length. Also, if North had held spade support he would have been able to raise pre-emptively.

Anyway, what penalty do you think the Italian maestros managed to extract?

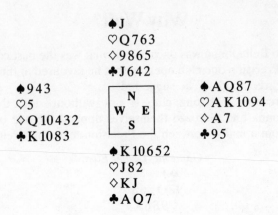

```
              ♠ J
              ♡ Q 7 6 3
              ◇ 9 8 6 5
              ♣ J 6 4 2
♠ 9 4 3                        ♠ A Q 8 7
♡ 5            ┌─────────┐      ♡ A K 1 0 9 4
◇ Q 1 0 4 3 2  │   N     │      ◇ A 7
♣ K 1 0 8 3    │ W     E │      ♣ 9 5
               │   S     │
               └─────────┘
              ♠ K 1 0 6 5 2
              ♡ J 8 2
              ◇ K J
              ♣ A Q 7
```

After a heart lead, followed by a club to the king and a club continuation, declarer led a trump to the jack and queen. Ace of hearts and a heart ruff, followed by a club ruff, led to this position:

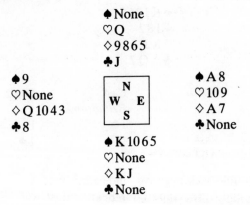

```
              ♠ None
              ♡ Q
              ◇ 9 8 6 5
              ♣ J
♠ 9                            ♠ A 8
♡ None         ┌─────────┐      ♡ 1 0 9
◇ Q 1 0 4 3    │   N     │      ◇ A 7
♣ 8            │ W     E │      ♣ None
               │   S     │
               └─────────┘
              ♠ K 1 0 6 5
              ♡ None
              ◇ K J
              ♣ None
```

East led a heart and declarer ruffed with the ten. At this point Garozzo underruffed with the nine! This spirited unblock allowed declarer's trump exit to run to East's eight. Belladonna then cashed the ace of spades and exited in hearts, forcing declarer to lead away from his diamonds. That was 1100 and a warning not to enter lightly against a strong club, not to mention strong opponents.

Close Encounter

There is a ghoulish fascination in those hands where the (modern) bidding is beyond all conceivable imagination. Consider this deal from an Olympiad match between the old rivals, Britain and Ireland.

Game all; Dealer West.

```
                    ♠Q653
                    ♡87
                    ◇KQ6
                    ♣AJ87
  ♠AK984                        ♠J1072
  ♡J4          N                ♡93
  ◇10      W       E            ◇97542
  ♣K10543       S               ♣Q2
                    ♠None
                    ♡AKQ10652
                    ◇AJ83
                    ♣96
```

At the first table the Irish North was unwontedly bashful.

West	North	East	South
Brock	*Senior*	*Forrester*	*Boland*
1♠	Pass	2♠	4♡
Pass	Pass [1]	Pass	

[1] He has some excellent cards, worth at least five hearts, if not six.

South made twelve tricks, of course.

At the other table the East-West pair had a method whereby an opening two hearts denoted a sub-standard major-minor two-suiter. What do you suppose happened there?

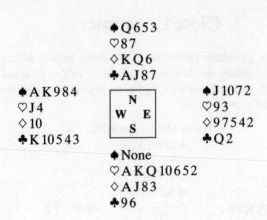

```
                    ♠ Q653
                    ♡ 87
                    ◇ KQ6
                    ♣ AJ87
  ♠ AK984        ┌─────┐      ♠ J1072
  ♡ J4           │  N  │      ♡ 93
  ◇ 10           │W   E│      ◇ 97542
  ♣ K10543       │  S  │      ♣ Q2
                 └─────┘
                    ♠ None
                    ♡ AKQ10652
                    ◇ AJ83
                    ♣ 96
```

This was the sequence when the Irish were East-West:

West	North	East	South
Mesbur	*Armstrong*	*Fitzgibbon*	*Kirby*
2♡[1]	Pass	Pass[2]	Pass[3]

[1] Denoting, as we said, a limited and unspecified major-minor two-suiter.

[2] From his angle, partner is more likely to hold hearts than spades.

[3] He could bid game in hearts or allow the vulnerable opponents to toil in two hearts. He chose the latter, if only because it seemed a rare opportunity to defend with such a trump holding.

The defence was well played. North led the king of diamonds and South overtook (North would hardly have led a king from Kx against such a contract). After drawing trumps South led a low diamond and his side made the first twelve tricks, for a penalty of 700 and an exciting gain of 1 IMP.

Youthful Impetuosity

One deal from the semi-final of the 1987 Bermuda Bowl attracted a *great* deal of comment, some of it pretty silly. See what you think of the various calls made on this deal from the match between Britain and Sweden.

Game all; Dealer East.

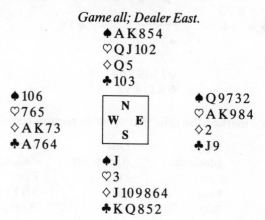

                    ♠ A K 8 5 4
                    ♡ Q J 10 2
                    ◇ Q 5
                    ♣ 10 3

    ♠ 10 6   ♠ Q 9 7 3 2
    ♡ 7 6 5   N   ♡ A K 9 8 4
    ◇ A K 7 3   W   E   ◇ 2
    ♣ A 7 6 4   S   ♣ J 9

                    ♠ J
                    ♡ 3
                    ◇ J 10 9 8 6 4
                    ♣ K Q 8 5 2

West	North	East	South
Forrester	*Lindqvist*	*Armstrong*	*Fallenius*
		2 NT	Pass
3 ♡	Pass	Pass	3 NT
Double	Pass	Pass	Redouble
All Pass			

This cost 2800 and a swing of 21 match points to Britain.

East's two no-trump opening was systemic, showing two suits excluding clubs, and 7-10 points. Whatever the artistic impression, we shall have to accept this call. But what of the others, on both sides? Which were debatable, which were frightful?

67

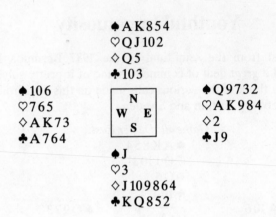

```
                    ♠AK854
                    ♡QJ102
                    ◇Q5
                    ♣103
        ♠106           N           ♠Q9732
        ♡765        W     E        ♡AK984
        ◇AK73          S           ◇2
        ♣A764                      ♣J9
                    ♠J
                    ♡3
                    ◇J109864
                    ♣KQ852
```

We have marked the calls that seem to require comment.

West	North	East	South
Forrester	*Lindqvist*	*Armstrong*	*Fallenius*
		2NT	Pass
3♡(1)	Pass	Pass	3NT(2)
Double	Pass	Pass	Redouble(3)
Pass	Pass(4)	Pass	

(1) This is reasonable, since if partner has diamonds and spades he will bid three spades and you can remove to four diamonds. However, three diamonds is somewhat safer. If partner removes this to three hearts you can pass.

(2) This was absurdly risky. Opponents are not even in game and you are forcing your side to the four level, with no assurance of a fit.

(3) No doubt he expected a rescue, but there was a *slight* danger that partner would pass and four diamonds would have been a safer choice.

(4) Well, he has a fair hand! This pass attracted most of the brickbats, but his partner might have been quite a bit stronger.

Moderate Consolation

Some of the bidding and play in the 96-board final of the 1988 Olympiad between Austria and the USA was quite awful. The schedule of three 20-board matches a day for a fortnight was excessive, particularly because it wasn't just a question of winning or losing a match — the struggle to score victory points was continuous.

Many of the worst mistakes were made in the first session. Look at this early board:

North-South game; Dealer West.

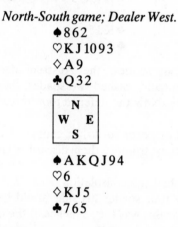

♠862
♡KJ1093
◇A9
♣Q32

♠AKQJ94
♡6
◇KJ5
♣765

West	North	East	South
Deutsch	*Kudlec*	*Wolff*	*Terraneo*
Pass	Pass	1◇	2♠
Pass	4♠	All Pass	

West led a low diamond to the queen and king. The declarer drew two rounds of trumps, finding them 2–2, then led a heart to the king. Anything wrong with that?

This was the full layout:

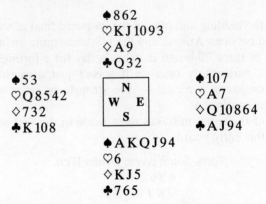

```
                    ♠862
                    ♡KJ1093
                    ◇A9
                    ♣Q32
    ♠53                          ♠107
    ♡Q8542          N            ♡A7
    ◇732         W     E         ◇Q10864
    ♣K108           S            ♣AJ94
                    ♠AKQJ94
                    ♡6
                    ◇KJ5
                    ♣765
```

Playing in four spades, the Austrian declarer won the diamond lead in hand, cashed two spades, then led a heart to the king and ace. Now the defence took three club tricks, for one down.

All the declarer needs to do, of course, is cross to the ace of diamonds, draw trumps, then discard a club on the jack of diamonds.

The declarer had the consolation, such as it was, that even if he had made four spades his side would have lost heavily on the board, for this was the sequence at the other table:

West	North	East	South
Fucik	*Meckstroth*	*Kubak*	*Rodwell*
1◇[1]	1♡	2◇	Double[2]
4◇	Pass	5◇[3]	Double
All Pass			

[1] Signifying 0-11 points (such is life nowadays).
[2] One of those negative doubles.
[3] Criminal; his partner's raise to four diamonds was purely defensive.

This was five down, 1100. The defence began with three rounds of diamonds and West later misguessed the queen of clubs.

Part 5

Technique in Attack

Some hands where the declarer had an unusual
problem, sometimes well managed at the table,
sometimes not.

Two Roundabout Ways

On this hand from a 1954 Gold Cup match both teams reached a dubious slam.

East-West game; Dealer North.

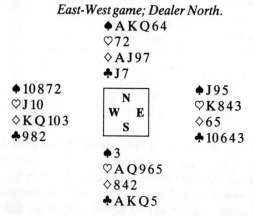

```
                ♠ A K Q 6 4
                ♡ 7 2
                ◇ A J 9 7
                ♣ J 7
  ♠ 10 8 7 2                      ♠ J 9 5
  ♡ J 10          N              ♡ K 8 4 3
  ◇ K Q 10 3    W   E            ◇ 6 5
  ♣ 9 8 2          S             ♣ 10 6 4 3
                ♠ 3
                ♡ A Q 9 6 5
                ◇ 8 4 2
                ♣ A K Q 5
```

In one room South played in six no-trumps on a club lead. The best line is to play on hearts, finessing the nine and then the queen. You need a 3–3 heart break and East to hold ♡Kxx or ♡J10x. Less good, but successful as the cards lie, is to finesse the the queen of hearts and play for three diamond tricks, hoping to find West with the ten and at least one of the high honours.

The original declarer embarked on a different tack. He won the lead with the ace of clubs and led a diamond, ducking West's king. He won the spade return, cashed the jack of clubs and finessed the queen of hearts. A successful finesse of the jack of diamonds was followed by king and queen of spades, ace of hearts and the remaining clubs, squeezing West in spades and diamonds.

No doubt South hoped for a big swing after his unorthodox play. In fact South in the other room made a still more unlikely slam, six hearts. Can you see how?

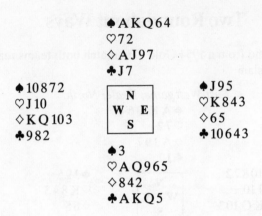

West led the king of diamonds against South's six hearts. Declarer won with the ace and cashed three top spades, disposing of his diamond losers. A diamond ruff in the South hand was followed by a club to the jack and another diamond lead from dummy. East could do no better than discard a club and South ruffed again. After cashing the ace of clubs declarer ruffed the king of clubs in dummy. This was the end position:

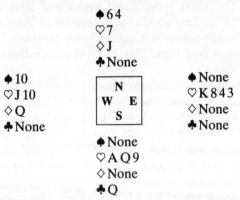

East had no answer to the jack of diamonds. If he ruffed low, declarer would overruff with the nine and exit in clubs, waiting to win the last two tricks with the ace and queen of hearts. It would be striking play for East to ruff with the king, but this doesn't work either; declarer would discard his club and score the last three tricks in the trump suit.

Five–One Not Fatal

In the Gold Cup final of 1954 L. Tarlo met Kempson, both teams studded with internationals. There was a big swing on this deal:

Love all; Dealer West.

♠ 10 4
♡ A 9 7
◇ 10 5 4 2
♣ Q 10 7 5

```
    N
 W     E
    S
```

♠ K Q J 9 8
♡ Q 8
◇ A K Q 9 8 7
♣ None

West	North	East	South
Cotter	*Franklin*	*Pearlstone*	*Tarlo*
1♡	Pass	2♡	3♡
4◇	Double	4♡	4♠
All Pass			

Louis Tarlo could guess that West's diamond bid was spurious but no doubt he was worried that there might be three top losers in a diamond contract.

West led the jack of hearts against four spades. It seemed to declarer that if he lost the first trick to East's king of hearts a club return would cause him to lose control when trumps were 4–2. He therefore called for dummy's ace of hearts.

Do you think that was a good idea?

This was the complete deal:

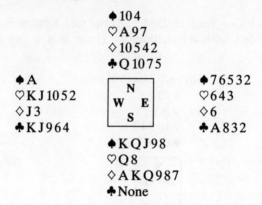

        ♠ 10 4
        ♡ A 9 7
        ◇ 10 5 4 2
        ♣ Q 10 7 5

♠ A   ♠ 7 6 5 3 2
♡ K J 10 5 2   N   ♡ 6 4 3
◇ J 3   W   E   ◇ 6
♣ K J 9 6 4   S   ♣ A 8 3 2

        ♠ K Q J 9 8
        ♡ Q 8
        ◇ A K Q 9 8 7
        ♣ None

West led the jack of hearts against four spades and Tarlo rose with the ace. When trumps proved to be 5–1 he lost control of the hand and went three down.

Declarer's play at trick one could hardly be criticised, but it is possible to construct an argument the other way. If West had held ♣ A K would he not have led a club? So, there was a fairly strong inference that West held the king of hearts for his opening bid. If South runs the heart lead to his queen he can overcome the poor trump division. Suppose that West switches to a club when he wins with the ace of spades. Dummy's ten forces the ace. Declarer can succeed by discarding a diamond; if another club is returned he discards a second diamond. He can then win the return and draw trumps.

This was the bidding in the other room:

West	North	East	South
Gardener	*Pavlides*	*Rose*	*Mathieson*
1♡	Pass	2♡	3♡
5♡	Double	Pass	6◇
All Pass			

Mathieson's six-diamond bid, as it turned out, was an excellent decision. When the jack of hearts was led the declarer had no option but to run it and the slam was made.

No Entry!

A curious deal arose in the 1959 European Championship. Great Britain were playing Austria and both sides reached three no-trumps on the North-South cards.

Game all; Dealer South.

♠KJ106
♡A86
◇K9753
♣10

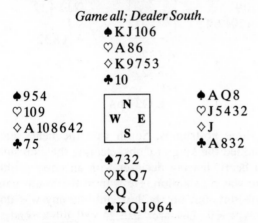

♠954
♡109
◇A108642
♣75

♠AQ8
♡J5432
◇J
♣A832

♠732
♡KQ7
◇Q
♣KQJ964

In the open room Reese played three no-trumps from the North seat and had an easy ride after the uninspired opening lead of the ace of spades.

In the closed room the Austrian South played three no-trumps on the lead of the ten of hearts. The contract seems indestructible, with five club tricks, three hearts, and surely a ninth trick from either diamonds or spades. Can you see the problem declarer ran into?

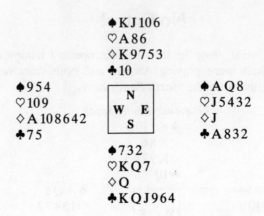

```
            ♠KJ106
            ♡A86
            ◇K9753
            ♣10
♠954                        ♠AQ8
♡109          N            ♡J5432
◇A108642    W   E          ◇J
♣75            S           ♣A832
            ♠732
            ♡KQ7
            ◇Q
            ♣KQJ964
```

Playing three no-trumps, South won the heart lead with the king and led the king of clubs, clearing the club suit. East returned a heart, leaving declarer with an entry problem to which there was no solution. He won in the South hand and ran the club suit, but on the last club dummy was down to ♠KJ10 ♡A ◇K9. Declarer had to call for a spade. Now when he led the queen of diamonds from hand, West won and switched to a spade. East cashed three tricks in the suit to put the game one down.

"Isn't it better to win the first heart in dummy and then overtake the ten of clubs?" North suggested.

This may look better, but observe the end position when the last club is led:

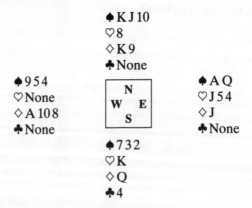

```
            ♠KJ10
            ♡8
            ◇K9
            ♣None
♠954                        ♠AQ
♡None         N            ♡J54
◇A108       W   E          ◇J
♣None          S           ♣None
            ♠732
            ♡K
            ◇Q
            ♣4
```

The ninth trick is still elusive.

Nothing to Choose?

The North-South cards on the deal below, from the 1961 *Daily Telegraph* Cup, offered two problems — one in the bidding, one in the play. The South player, Harrison-Gray, managed to solve them both.

Love all; Dealer South.

♠Q9754
♡QJ
◇J63
♣Q74

```
    N
 W     E
    S
```

♠AK
♡94
◇A72
♣AKJ652

West	North	East	South
	Flint		Gray
			1♣
Pass	1♠	Pass	2◇
Pass	3♣	Pass	3♡
Pass	3 NT	Pass	5♣
All Pass			

Most players would pass three no-trumps, hoping that North had a secure heart stop. Harrison-Gray advanced to five clubs, taking the view that something as modest as ♠QJxx ♣Qxx opposite would make this contract secure. After the ace of hearts lead and a heart to East's king, East switched to the king of diamonds, South winning with the ace. Declarer played one round of trumps and two rounds of spades, both defenders following all the way. Two lines are possible now. What are they, and which is better?

This was the complete deal:

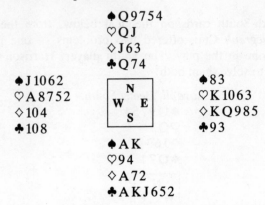

```
                ♠Q9754
                ♡QJ
                ◇J63
                ♣Q74
♠J1062                        ♠83
♡A8752      N                 ♡K1063
◇104      W   E              ◇KQ985
♣108          S              ♣93
                ♠AK
                ♡94
                ◇A72
                ♣AKJ652
```

The defence against five clubs started with ace of hearts, king of hearts, and king of diamonds, won by the ace. Gray drew one round of trumps with the ace, then cashed the ace and king of spades, drawing small cards from the defenders. There were two possible lines now. If spades were 3–3 he could afford to play the king and queen of trumps before turning to the spades. Alternatively, if trumps were 2–2, he could cross to the queen of clubs on the second round of trumps, ruff the spades good, and return to dummy with a third round of trumps to the seven.

There is little to choose mathematically between the remaining spades being 1–1 and the remaining clubs being 1–1. Gray went for the latter chance and made the contract.

Was this merely a lucky choice? No, Gray realised that if he played for an even trump break and *East* turned up with three trumps, he would still make the contract when the spades were 3–3. This made the line he chose easily the best shot.

Trump to Spare

It is strange how much you can do when you have an abundance of trumps in each hand. This deal is from a match between France and Norway in the European Championship.

Game all; Dealer South.

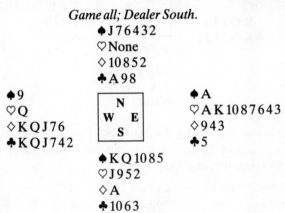

♠J76432
♡None
◇10852
♣A98

♠9
♡Q
◇KQJ76
♣KQJ742

♠A
♡AK1087643
◇943
♣5

♠KQ1085
♡J952
◇A
♣1063

This was the bidding when Norway was East-West:

West	North	East	South
			Pass
1◇	1♠	3♡	4♠
4NT	Pass	5♡	All Pass

This had to go one down. At the other table:

West	North	East	South
			1♠
2NT	4♠	5♡	Pass
Pass	5♠	Double	All Pass

West led the queen of hearts. It looks as though declarer must lose three tricks — a trump and two clubs. Can it be made nevertheless? Would a trump lead be better for the defence?

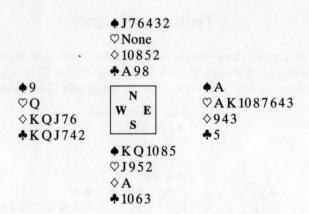

♠J76432
♡None
◇10852
♣A98

♠9
♡Q
◇KQJ76
♣KQJ742

N
W E
S

♠A
♡AK1087643
◇943
♣5

♠KQ1085
♡J952
◇A
♣1063

Playing in five spades doubled, Ulf Tundal ruffed the heart lead, crossed to the ace of diamonds, and cross-ruffed the red suits to reach this ending:

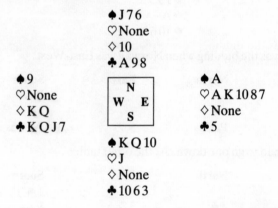

♠J76
♡None
◇10
♣A98

♠9
♡None
◇KQ
♣KQJ7

N
W E
S

♠A
♡AK1087
◇None
♣5

♠KQ10
♡J
◇None
♣1063

Now a club to the ace, diamond ruff, and the jack of hearts, discarding a club from dummy. (If West ruffs the fourth heart dummy overruffs and East is left on play with the ace of spades.)

"I suppose we can beat it if you lead a trump," said East sadly.

But no! Again South can ruff three hearts and two diamonds, cash ace of clubs, and finally lead the jack of hearts, discarding a club from dummy.

Polish Caviare

A slight surprise to pick up a two count, hear the bidding opened on your left, and finish as declarer in a slam contract!

North-South game; Dealer West.

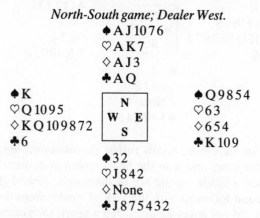

This was the bidding when Poland was North-South against Brazil in the 1984 Olympiad:

West	North	East	South
1◇	Double	1♠	Pass
2◇	Double	Pass	4♣
Pass	6♣	All Pass	

West led the king of diamonds and Przybora ruffed. The club finesse lost and a heart was returned, won in dummy. Declarer cashed the ace of diamonds, discarding a spade, and then the ace of spades (it was certain that West would have an honour in spades after East had shown up with the king of clubs.)

Can you see how the play continues?

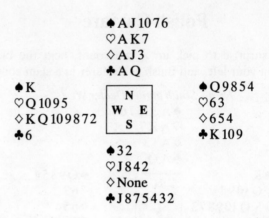

$\spadesuit$AJ1076
$\heartsuit$AK7
$\diamond$AJ3
$\clubsuit$AQ

$\spadesuit$K
$\heartsuit$Q1095
$\diamond$KQ109872
$\clubsuit$6

$\spadesuit$Q9854
$\heartsuit$63
$\diamond$654
$\clubsuit$K109

$\spadesuit$32
$\heartsuit$J842
$\diamond$None
$\clubsuit$J875432

Playing in six clubs, South ruffed the diamond lead, lost a club to the king, and won the heart return in dummy. Then he discarded a spade on the ace of diamonds, cashed the ace of spades, and followed with the jack of spades from dummy. When East did not cover he discarded a heart, then cashed the ace of clubs, came to hand with a spade ruff, and played off all the trumps. At the finish West, holding $\heartsuit$Q10 and $\diamond$Q, was squeezed in front of dummy's $\heartsuit$K7 and $\diamond$J.

Perhaps you wondered why Przybora did not cash the ace of clubs before leading the second spade from dummy. There was an excellent reason. If he cashes the club and follows with the jack of spades, East may cover. South will ruff, draw the remaining trumps, and cross to the king of hearts to cash the ten of spades. But now the squeeze doesn't work, because dummy has no entry card. It was top-class play by the declarer.

Brazilian Spot-Kick

Sometimes when you watch a top expert at work he will make a seemingly inexplicable move. Why did he do that, you wonder. This was such a hand, from the 1984 World Teams Olympiad. Brazil was facing Canada and the Brazilian ace, Marcelo Branco, was in the South seat.

East-West game; Dealer South.

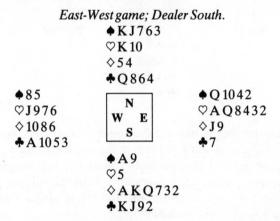

♠KJ763
♡K10
◇54
♣Q864

♠85
♡J976
◇1086
♣A1053

♠Q1042
♡AQ8432
◇J9
♣7

♠A9
♡5
◇AKQ732
♣KJ92

Branco ended in five clubs after an auction in which East had indicated his hearts. West duly led a heart and declarer ruffed the second round of the suit. The king and jack of clubs were allowed to hold. Another round of trumps would be fatal, since West would win and force dummy's last trump with another round of hearts. (South has used one of his trumps to ruff, you remember.)

How did Branco proceed from this point?

This was the position when Branco made his key play:

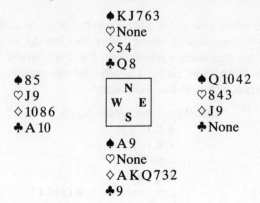

♠KJ763
♡None
♢54
♣Q8

♠85   ♠Q1042
♡J9   N   ♡843
       W   E
♢1086   S   ♢J9
♣A10   ♣None

♠A9
♡None
♢AKQ732
♣9

If declarer simply runs his diamonds at this stage, West will discard his spades and score two of the last three tricks.

Suppose instead that declarer cashes the ace and king of spades, then starts on the diamonds. West will ruff the fourth round with the ace and exit with the ten of clubs; there will then be a spade loser in dummy.

In the diagram position Branco played a spade to the king and then proceeded to run the diamonds. West was powerless. If he refused to ruff, declarer would discard all four of dummy's remaining spades. If West instead chose to ruff high and exit with his last trump (or give a ruff-and-discard), the spade ace would give declarer an entry to the remaining diamonds. It was great play.

Of Dubious Value

The Lightner slam double, requesting partner to make an unexpected lead, has already passed its Golden Jubilee and is played by "everyone". The idea has also spread to game contracts. But what would the answer be if the results could be analysed of all the Lightner doubles that have been made since the beginning of time? On the one side the brilliant successes, on the other the times when the lead wasn't necessary, or when it wasn't enough to beat the contract, or when it drove the opposition into a better contract. This example is from the 1988 Olympiad.

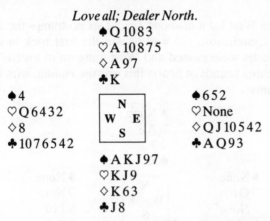

Love all; Dealer North.

```
                    ♠Q1083
                    ♡A10875
                    ◇A97
                    ♣K
  ♠4                            ♠652
  ♡Q6432         N              ♡None
  ◇8           W   E            ◇QJ10542
  ♣1076542       S              ♣AQ93
                    ♠AKJ97
                    ♡KJ9
                    ◇K63
                    ♣J8
```

With Iceland North-South against Australia the bidding went:

West	North	East	South
	2♡[1]	3◇	4NT
Pass	5♡	Pass	6♠
Pass	Pass	Double	6NT[2]
All Pass			

[1] A type of Flannery, denoting 4–4 or 4–5 in the majors.
[2] It was easy to judge that the double was Lightner, asking for a heart lead.

What should West lead? A club, no doubt (for five down). But he led his partner's suit, a diamond. What do you suppose happened then? South has only eleven tricks on top.

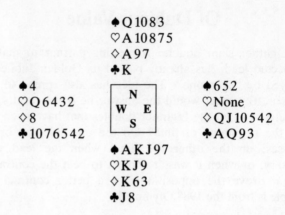

♠Q1083
♡A10875
◇A97
♣K

♠4　　　　　　　　　♠652
♡Q6432　　　　　　♡None
◇8　　　　　　　　　◇QJ10542
♣1076542　　　　　♣AQ93

♠AKJ97
♡KJ9
◇K63
♣J8

When West led a diamond against six no-trumps the declarer, Bjorn Eysteinsson, did well to win the first trick in dummy. The spades were cashed and West hung on to his five hearts. After three rounds of hearts this was the ending, with the lead in dummy:

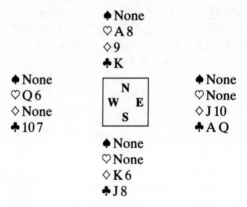

♠None
♡A8
◇9
♣K

♠None　　　　　　　♠None
♡Q6　　　　　　　　♡None
◇None　　　　　　　◇J10
♣107　　　　　　　　♣AQ

♠None
♡None
◇K6
♣J8

On the ace of hearts East did his best, discarding the queen of clubs. A club followed and South made the twelfth trick with the jack of clubs.

At the time some pundits suggested that East should have made a second Lightner double, of six no-trumps. Since this contract was presumably something of a step into the dark, though, the meaning of a double might have been unclear.

High Dive

You may think that your partnership has locked all the doors and shut all the windows, but every now and again a seemingly insoluble bidding problem may arise. This was South's predicament on a deal from the 1988 Vanderbilt semi-finals. He held:

♠ A Q J 6
♡ None
♢ A K Q 3
♣ A K Q 8 4

The bidding began:

West	North	East	South
			1♣[1]
Pass	2♡[2]	Pass	2NT[3]
Pass	3♡[4]	Pass	?

[1] Precision Club, 16+ points.
[2] Six hearts, 3-6 points.
[3] Asking for more information.
[4] No feature to show outside hearts.

What would your next move have been?

The original South player gave up on any further constructive moves, leaping to six clubs. The auction continued Pass, Pass, Double. Would you stick this or move to some alternative contract?

South decided to try his luck in six clubs doubled. This was the full deal:

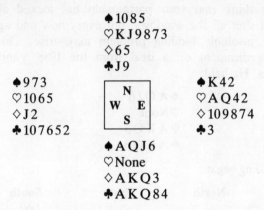

```
                    ♠1085
                    ♡KJ9873
                    ◇65
                    ♣J9
    ♠973                         ♠K42
    ♡1065          N             ♡AQ42
    ◇J2         W     E          ◇109874
    ♣107652        S             ♣3
                    ♠AQJ6
                    ♡None
                    ◇AKQ3
                    ♣AKQ84
```

The main reason for East's Lightner double was that it would prevent West from leading a spade. West duly led a heart, as instructed. The jack from dummy was covered by the queen and ruffed by declarer. South continued with ace and king of diamonds and ruffed a diamond, West discarding a spade. Next came the ten of spades from dummy, which won, and a spade to the jack. These cards remained:

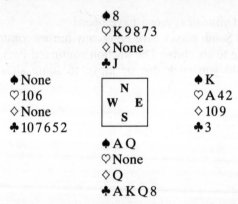

```
                    ♠8
                    ♡K9873
                    ◇None
                    ♣J
    ♠None                       ♠K
    ♡106           N            ♡A42
    ◇None       W     E         ◇109
    ♣107652        S            ♣3
                    ♠AQ
                    ♡None
                    ◇Q
                    ♣AKQ8
```

West had no answer when the queen of diamonds was led. If he ruffed, declarer would overruff in the dummy and play a spade. Whether or not West ruffed the spade, declarer would be in control. Nor would it help West to discard on the queen of diamonds. Declarer would simply lead his good spades.

Swiss Miss

In the 1988 European Championship the British ladies defeated Switzerland by a staggering 120-5. This deal contributed handsomely.

East-West game; Dealer North.

      ♠ A 6 3 2
      ♡ A
      ◊ J 5 4
      ♣ A K Q 6 5

```
        N
    W       E
        S
```

      ♠ K
      ♡ 8 6 3 2
      ◊ A K 9 6 2
      ♣ J 9 2

The Swiss North-South suffered a common type of bidding misunderstanding:

West	North	East	South
Smith	*Fierz*	*Davies*	*Moretti*
	1♣	Pass	1◊
Pass	1♠	Pass	2♡
Pass	3◊	All Pass	

Obviously North and her partner had different ideas about how far a fourth-suit bid should be forcing.

The British auction was hardly ideal either:

West	North	East	South
Varenne	*Bethe*	*Dumorteil*	*Shaw*
	1♣	Pass	1◊
Pass	1♠	Pass	2 NT
Pass	4 NT	Pass	5◊
Pass	6◊	All Pass	

There is little point in Blackwood, since ◊ K Q 10 x x in the South hand would be more useful than ◊ A x x x x. Still, the contract was a good one. How would you play it (a) on a spade lead, (b) on a heart lead?

The full deal was as follows:

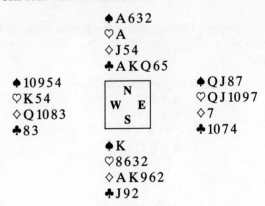

```
                    ♠ A 6 3 2
                    ♡ A
                    ◇ J 5 4
                    ♣ A K Q 6 5
    ♠ 10 9 5 4                          ♠ Q J 8 7
    ♡ K 5 4          N                  ♡ Q J 10 9 7
    ◇ Q 10 8 3    W     E               ◇ 7
    ♣ 8 3            S                  ♣ 10 7 4
                    ♠ K
                    ♡ 8 6 3 2
                    ◇ A K 9 6 2
                    ♣ J 9 2
```

Liza Shaw received a spade lead, and proceeded to make the contract with a neat safety play in trumps. She crossed to the ace of trumps and led a low trump towards the jack. West was held to just one trump trick and the slam was made.

The play is more interesting on a heart lead. Declarer must cross to the king of spades and lead a low diamond to the jack (not ace and another, because then another heart from West will be fatal). If West plays low (best), declarer must duck the next round of trumps. There is still a trump left in dummy to protect declarer from a further attack in hearts.

Warning Beacon

The borderline slam hand below arose in the 1989 Tollemache Cup. Hampshire, North-South at this table, was facing Cambridgeshire.

```
            ♠Q5
            ♡AK8
            ◇QJ72
            ♣AKJ7
         ┌─────────┐
         │   N     │
         │ W   E   │
         │   S     │
         └─────────┘
            ♠KJ82
            ♡QJ1093
            ◇A8
            ♣85
```

West	North	East	South
Tony	David	Brian	Richard
Forrester	Bird	Senior	Hyde
	2◇¹	Pass	2♡²
Pass	2NT	Pass	3◇³
Pass	3♡	Pass	3♠
Pass	4♣	Pass	4◇
Double	4♡	Pass	4NT⁴
Pass	5♣⁵	Pass	6♡
All Pass			

¹ Multi-coloured two diamonds, here a natural two no-trumps opening.
² At first responder allows for the weak type.
³ Transfer bid.
⁴ Roman Key-card Blackwood.
⁵ Three of the five 'aces'.

West leads the six of clubs, taken by the ace. At trick two dummy's queen of spades is taken by East's ace and East returns the four of diamonds. West's double of your diamond cue bid hardly makes a diamond finesse a healthy prospect. What line would you take?

This was the complete deal:

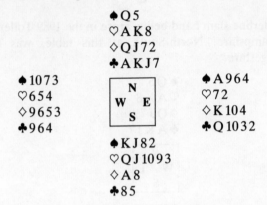

```
                  ♠ Q 5
                  ♡ A K 8
                  ◇ Q J 7 2
                  ♣ A K J 7
♠ 1073                              ♠ A 9 6 4
♡ 654         ┌──────────┐         ♡ 7 2
◇ 9653        │    N     │         ◇ K 10 4
♣ 964         │  W   E   │         ♣ Q 10 3 2
              │    S     │
              └──────────┘
                  ♠ K J 8 2
                  ♡ Q J 10 9 3
                  ◇ A 8
                  ♣ 8 5
```

West, who had doubled a four-diamond cue-bid during the auction, led the six of clubs against South's six hearts. Declarer won with the ace of clubs and played the queen of spades, taken by East's ace. When East played the four of diamonds the declarer, Richard Hyde, blithely ran this to dummy's ◇ Q J. He could then ruff a spade high, draw trumps and claim the contract.

What inspired this cavalier disregard of West's earlier double? Firstly, Tony Forrester has a well publicised liking for psychic lead-directing doubles. Secondly, the fact that Forrester himself would be on lead against a likely heart contract raised further doubt concerning the authenticity of the double.

Multinational

Here is a deal from the World Team event at Geneva in 1990, slightly misplayed by an American declarer against two Polish internationals, noted by a Russian (Tiit Laanemae) and reported by a Frenchman (Guy Dupont) in the Bulletin edited by an American (Henry Francis) and a Welshman (Patrick Jourdain).

East-West game; Dealer East.

♠ K 8 5 4
♡ A J 8 3 2
◇ Q 10
♣ 5 2

```
      N
  W       E
      S
```

♠ 3 2
♡ 5
◇ K J 9 7 6 4 2
♣ A Q 9

West	North	East	South
Tuszynski	*Martel*	*Kowalski*	*Stansby*
		2♣¹	2◇
2♡²	Pass	Pass	3◇
Double	All Pass		

¹ Club suit, not strong.
² Natural, not forcing.

West's lead of the ten of clubs ran to declarer's queen. How should South set about the play?

This was the complete deal:

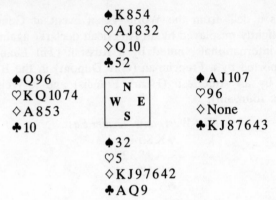

```
                    ♠ K854
                    ♡ AJ832
                    ◇ Q10
                    ♣ 52
  ♠ Q96              N           ♠ AJ107
  ♡ KQ1074     W         E       ♡ 96
  ◇ A853             S           ◇ None
  ♣ 10                           ♣ KJ87643
                    ♠ 32
                    ♡ 5
                    ◇ KJ97642
                    ♣ AQ9
```

Playing in three diamonds doubled after East had opened with a natural two clubs and West had bid hearts, South won the club lead with the queen and followed with the ace. Disaster! West ruffed and played ace and another diamond.

In the end South lost five tricks — two spades, ace of diamonds, a ruff, and the third round of clubs.

No doubt it did not occur to Stansby that the two-club opening might have been made on a seven-card suit. There was, of course, a safety play available — a *low* club from hand at trick two. If the opponents play two rounds of trumps now, you continue drawing trumps and lose just two spades, a diamond and a club. On any other defence declarer plays the ace of clubs and is able to overruff West.

The play is a variation of the well known situation where a player with A K x x x opposite x x in a side suit must not crack out the king on the second round when there is danger of a 5–1 break.

Part 6

Technique in Defence

Mostly occasions when a defender missed
a subtle point.

Winner on Loser

On this deal from a Ladies Trials match in 1954, declarer failed to play the hand to best advantage. Just as well, in the long run, because an interesting defensive position arose.

Love all; Dealer West.

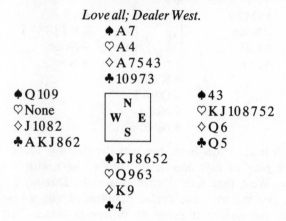

```
                  ♠A7
                  ♡A4
                  ◇A7543
                  ♣10973
  ♠Q109          N            ♠43
  ♡None      W       E        ♡KJ108752
  ◇J1082                      ◇Q6
  ♣AKJ862        S            ♣Q5
                  ♠KJ8652
                  ♡Q963
                  ◇K9
                  ♣4
```

West	North	East	South
1♣	1◇	3♡	3♠
Pass	4♠	All Pass	

West started with the ace of clubs and at trick two continued with a low club, ruffed by South. Declarer was on the right lines when she played the king and ace of diamonds (the fifth diamond can be established). Her next move, though, was to ruff a club in the South hand.

A low heart was now played towards the dummy. How do you think West should defend at this point?

This is the key moment for the defence:

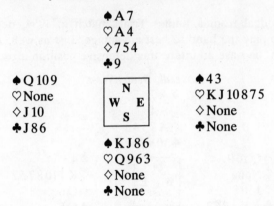

♠A7
♡A4
◇754
♣9

♠Q109   ♠43
♡None   ♡KJ10875
◇J10   ◇None
♣J86   ♣None

♠KJ86
♡Q963
◇None
♣None

South leads a low heart towards the dummy. Generally it is poor play to ruff one of declarer's losers with a trump winner. West therefore discarded a club. Dummy's ace of hearts won the trick and declarer continued with a low heart towards the queen. It made no difference which card East played. In fact she put in the jack, covered by the queen and ruffed by West. West could do no better than return a trump but declarer won with the jack, ruffed a heart with the ace and returned to hand to draw the last trump. Ten tricks made.

Strangely, if West does ruff in the diagram position, the contract cannot be made. Declarer ruffs the minor suit exit. If she draws trumps now she will have two heart losers at the end; if she doesn't draw trumps West will ruff the ace of hearts and exit with a trump. Declarer, with three tricks already lost, will have only one trump in the dummy to deal with two heart losers.

The King Was Lost

In 1957 the teams of Reese and Preston fought a series of matches to determine the team that would represent Great Britain in the World Championships. East faced a defensive problem on this deal.

Love all; Dealer West.

♠ 3
♡ K 4 2
◇ A J 9 8 5 3
♣ A 7 2

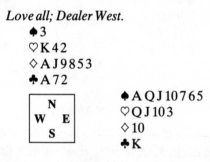

♠ A Q J 10 7 6 5
♡ Q J 10 3
◇ 10
♣ K

West	North	East	South
Schapiro	*Gardener*	*Reese*	*Rose*
Pass	1◇	3♠	3 NT
All Pass			

East's first problem was in the bidding. If the hand were offered to a bidding panel there would doubtless be votes for one, two, three or four spades.

Anyway, South ended in three no-trumps and West led the nine of spades. How would you plan the defence from the East seat?

This was the complete deal:

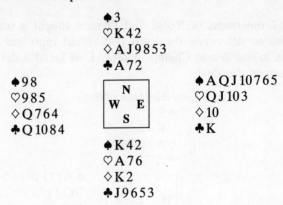

```
                  ♠ 3
                  ♡ K 4 2
                  ◇ A J 9 8 5 3
                  ♣ A 7 2
♠ 9 8                              ♠ A Q J 10 7 6 5
♡ 9 8 5           N                ♡ Q J 10 3
◇ Q 7 6 4      W     E             ◇ 10
♣ Q 10 8 4        S                ♣ K
                  ♠ K 4 2
                  ♡ A 7 6
                  ◇ K 2
                  ♣ J 9 6 5 3
```

East overtook the nine of spades with the ten and declarer had to duck. Since East had no outside entry it was clear that he could not bring in the spades. He therefore switched to the queen of hearts at trick two. Declarer won the heart switch with the king, crossed to the king of diamonds and finessed the jack. When East showed out, declarer cleared the diamond suit. West played back a heart and South could make no more than eight tricks.

The same contract was reached in the other room but here East allowed the nine of spades to hold. West, who could scarcely find the heart switch from his side of the table, continued with another spade. The contract was now made in comfort since West had no spade to return when the diamond suit was cleared. Declarer's king of spades which was never made in the other room, provided the game-going trick.

Accurate Expression

In the quarter-finals of the 1964 Gold Cup, Reese met the Yorkshire team of Rita Oldroyd. West's defence was put to the test on this deal:

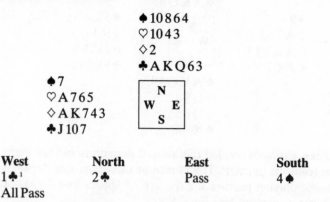

♠ 10864
♡ 1043
◇ 2
♣ A K Q 6 3

♠ 7
♡ A 7 6 5
◇ A K 7 4 3
♣ J 10 7

West	North	East	South
1♣[1]	2♣	Pass	4♠
All Pass			

[1] Little major system, in which one diamond signifies spades (or a strong no-trump) and one club signified hearts.

You lead the king of diamonds (your normal play from A K) and partner contributes the eight. What is your next move?

This was the full deal:

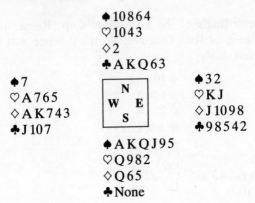

```
                    ♠ 10 8 6 4
                    ♡ 10 4 3
                    ◇ 2
                    ♣ A K Q 6 3
    ♠ 7                              ♠ 32
    ♡ A 7 6 5          N            ♡ K J
    ◇ A K 7 4 3     W     E         ◇ J 10 9 8
    ♣ J 10 7           S            ♣ 9 8 5 4 2
                    ♠ A K Q J 9 5
                    ♡ Q 9 8 2
                    ◇ Q 6 5
                    ♣ None
```

Reese, sitting West, led the king of diamonds and the eight came from his partner. The choice at this stage was between a trump, playing partner for the ace of spades and ♡ Q J, or a low heart, playing him for ♡ K x.

Since declarer was likely to hold solid spades on this bidding, West switched to the five of hearts. When East won with the king of hearts and returned the jack the Yorkshire declarer, Manning, played the eight. This was a good try but it was clear to West that declarer would have covered with ♡ Q x x. He therefore overtook the jack of hearts with the ace and gave his partner a ruff for the setting trick.

This was the strange-looking bidding in the other room:

West	North	East	South
	Konstam		*Rodrigue*
1◇	2◇[1]	Double	Pass (!)
Pass	2♠	Pass	4♠
All Pass			

[1] Showing a distributional double.

"The reason I passed," Rodrigue explained, "was that I expected partner to bid two hearts and I was going to raise this to five hearts." Ah, of course; we knew there must be a good reason.

East led the jack of diamonds against four spades and switched to the king of hearts. When he continued with the jack of hearts, Konstam read the situation and refrained from covering. West played low and the game was made.

Nearly Right

A small problem in defence from the other side of the globe — from a team event in Australia:

Game all; Dealer South.

♠ K 9 7 6 4 3
♡ A K 10 8 5
◇ None
♣ 10 8

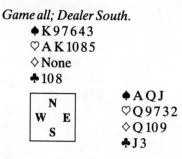

♠ A Q J
♡ Q 9 7 3 2
◇ Q 10 9
♣ J 3

The bidding has been:

West	North	East	South
			1♣
Pass	1♠	Pass	3♣
Pass	3♡	Pass	3 NT
Pass	4♡	Pass	5♣
Pass	6♣	All Pass	

West leads the two of spades, you win with the jack and South plays the ten.

You know that South has powerful clubs and a guard in diamonds. What do you lead at trick two?

You can be sure that the spade lead was from three small, not a singleton. You are not going to make any tricks in spades or hearts, so you must hope for a trick in diamonds. You must lead a trump now, that's for sure. East worked that out at the table, but he made a small error nevertheless. These were the four hands:

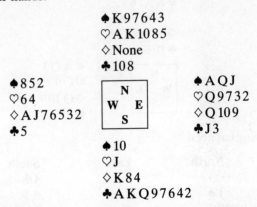

```
                    ♠K97643
                    ♡AK1085
                    ◇None
                    ♣108
   ♠852                              ♠AQJ
   ♡64           ┌─────────┐        ♡Q9732
   ◇AJ76532      │   N     │        ◇Q109
   ♣5            │ W   E   │        ♣J3
                 │   S     │
                 └─────────┘
                    ♠10
                    ♡J
                    ◇K84
                    ♣AKQ97642
```

Defending against six clubs, East won the first trick with the jack of spades and returned the three of clubs. The declarer, Andrew Davis, let this run to dummy's eight, ruffed a spade, ruffed a diamond, and ruffed another spade to establish the suit.

As you see, the *jack* of clubs from East at trick two was necessary to prevent this sequence.

Self-Mate

The chess maestro Bobby Fischer once wrote:
'You have thought of a good move. Bravo! But don't play too quickly. There may well be an even better move."
East should have thought of that when the following hand was played in the semi-final of an American team event:

Game all; Dealer South.

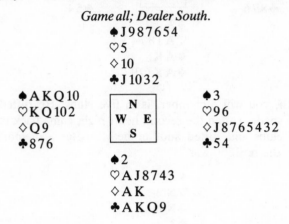

♠J987654
♡5
◇10
♣J1032

♠AKQ10
♡KQ102
◇Q9
♣876

♠3
♡96
◇J8765432
♣54

♠2
♡AJ8743
◇AK
♣AKQ9

West	North	East	South
			2♣
Pass	2◇	Pass	2♡
Pass	2♠	Pass	3♣
Pass	3♠	Pass	3NT
Pass	4♣	Pass	5♣
All Pass			

West began with two top spades and East discarded a heart on the second round. South ruffed, played ace of hearts and ruffed a heart with the ten of clubs. After a club to the ace he ruffed another heart with the jack of clubs.

West still has a master heart. Is South going to make his contract or not?

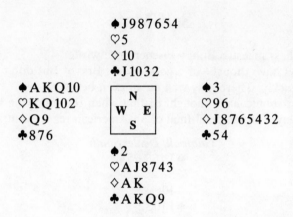

♠J987654
♡5
◇10
♣J1032

♠AKQ10   ♠3
♡KQ102   ♡96
◇Q9   ◇J8765432
♣876   ♣54

♠2
♡AJ8743
◇AK
♣AKQ9

South, you will remember, is in five clubs. He ruffed the second spade, ruffed the second heart high, came back to the ace of clubs and ruffed another heart. After a diamond to the ace the position was:

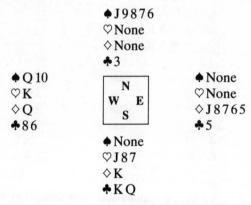

♠J9876
♡None
◇None
♣3

♠Q10   ♠None
♡K   ♡None
◇Q   ◇J8765
♣86   ♣5

♠None
♡J87
◇K
♣KQ

When the next heart was ruffed with the three of clubs East pounced on this with his five. An expensive mistake, as you can see. South won the diamond return and made the rest. If East declines to overruff, South must lose two more tricks.

At the other table North played in four spades. West did well not to double, because if North does everything right, playing West for four trumps, he might make this contract by way of a trump coup.

Hungarian Goulash

There were possibilities for both sides on this deal from the 1975 European Championship. Great Britain faced Hungary and Claude Rodrigue was sitting East.

```
            ♠873
            ♡J
            ◇AQJ8742
            ♣AQ
                        ♠A5
         N              ♡976
      W     E           ◇K9
         S              ♣1076432
```

West	North	East	South
			1♠
Pass	2◇ [1]	Pass	2♡
Pass	2♠	Pass	2NT
Pass	3◇	Pass	4♣
Pass	4♠	All Pass	

[1] Forcing to game in the Hungarian system.

West leads a trump and you win with the ace. Prospects are not especially bright. What do you plan to do?

This was the complete deal:

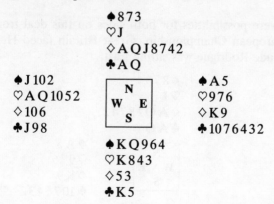

```
                 ♠ 8 7 3
                 ♡ J
                 ◇ A Q J 8 7 4 2
                 ♣ A Q
  ♠ J 10 2              N              ♠ A 5
  ♡ A Q 10 5 2      W       E          ♡ 9 7 6
  ◇ 10 6               S              ◇ K 9
  ♣ J 9 8                              ♣ 10 7 6 4 3 2
                 ♠ K Q 9 6 4
                 ♡ K 8 4 3
                 ◇ 5 3
                 ♣ K 5
```

Rodrigue, sitting East, won the trump lead with the ace and made the fine return of a heart, indirectly attacking dummy's trump holding. Priday, West, won with the queen and switched to a club. Declarer took the trick in dummy with the queen, played a spade to the king, and continued with a losing diamond finesse. Now another heart from East stranded him in the dummy with no way back to hand to draw the last trump.

Declarer does better to win the club switch with the king and finesse diamonds immediately. Now East cannot attack both the club and diamond entries to dummy.

110

Stuck in the Gate

Have you ever been end-played at trick one? It happened to the two West players when Taiwan (the winners) played Australia (the runners-up) in the 1976 Far East Championship. This was the deal:

```
                 ♠ 8 4 3
                 ♡ 10 3
                 ◇ Q J 5
                 ♣ K 9 7 4 3
              ┌─────────┐
              │    N    │
              │  W   E  │
              │    S    │
              └─────────┘
                 ♠ A K J 7 5 2
                 ♡ K J
                 ◇ A 9
                 ♣ A 10 8
```

West	North	East	South
Cheng	*Borin*	*Hsiao*	*Havas*
			1♠
Pass	2♣	Pass	4♠
All Pass			

West leads the two of diamonds and dummy's queen wins the trick. How do you play now?

This was the full layout:

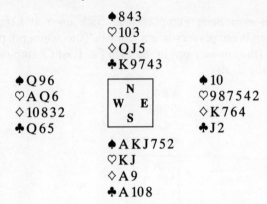

```
                    ♠843
                    ♡103
                    ◇QJ5
                    ♣K9743
♠Q96                 ┌─────┐        ♠10
♡AQ6                 │  N  │        ♡987542
◇10832               │W   E│        ◇K764
♣Q65                 │  S  │        ♣J2
                     └─────┘
                    ♠AKJ752
                    ♡KJ
                    ◇A9
                    ♣A108
```

In both rooms West led the two of diamonds against four spades, East correctly allowing dummy's queen to win. Let's see first how the Taiwanese South tackled the hand. He started with the ace, king and another trump. In with the trump queen, West exited safely with a diamond. Declarer cashed the ace of clubs and ran the ten to East's jack. When a heart came through, declarer was one down.

George Havas, the Australian declarer, played differently at trick two. Instead of drawing trumps he played a club to the ten. With dummy's club suit established, West rightly tried ace and another heart. Declarer had to lose a trump to West but made the rest of the tricks, ten in all.

The line chosen by Havas might have fared poorly if East had held a low singleton club. It catered for several other situations, though, such as East holding ♠Qxx and three clubs to an honour.

As we remarked at the beginning, West was effectively end-played at trick one. Every lead would concede a trick, one way or another.

I Told You..

This defensive situation arose in a match from the 1976 *Sunday Times* tournament. You are sitting East.

Game all; Dealer East.

♠ Q 7
♡ J 6 5 3
◇ A 6 3
♣ K 10 7 3

```
         N
       W   E
         S
```

♠ 10 9 5 4 2
♡ K Q 9
◇ 10 4
♣ Q J 4

West	North	East	South
		Pass	1 NT
Pass	3 NT	All Pass	

You win the two of hearts lead with the nine and continue with the king and queen, partner following with the seven and the ten. The one no-trump opening promised 14-16 points, so West will hold between 2-4 points in addition to the ace of hearts. What switch do you make at trick four?

This was the complete deal:

Game all; Dealer East.

♠Q7
♡J653
◇A63
♣K1073

♠J83
♡A1072
◇QJ72
♣86

♠109542
♡KQ9
◇104
♣QJ4

♠AK6
♡84
◇K985
♣A952

At the table East switched to a spade, perhaps hoping to blast a hole to partner's king of spades while the clubs were still under control. Declarer won with the ace and ducked a club to East, the safe hand. Declarer had eight tricks now and West was subsequently squeezed in the red suits to yield a ninth.

If East switches to a diamond at trick four, and plays another diamond when he takes his club trick, the squeeze is broken. What clue was available to East? If West had wanted a spade switch he would have played the ten of hearts followed by the seven on the second and third rounds of the suit. His actual play of the seven followed by the ten should have been interpreted as an indication that he did not hold a high spade.

Under the Table

This spectacular hand arose in a clash between the British and Belgian ladies. A poor opening lead by the Belgian West set her partner an impossible defensive problem.

Game all; Dealer South.

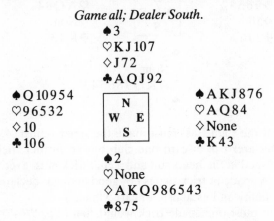

♠3
♥KJ107
♦J72
♣AQJ92

♠Q10954
♥96532
♦10
♣106

♠AKJ876
♥AQ84
♦None
♣K43

♠2
♥None
♦AKQ986543
♣875

West	North	East	South
			5♦
Pass	Pass	5♠	Pass
Pass	6♦	Double	All Pass

West led the five of spades to partner's king and East had an unattractive return at trick two. She eventually tried to cash the ace of hearts but declarer ruffed and was able to establish a second club discard on dummy's heart suit.

Do you see how East could have beaten the slam?

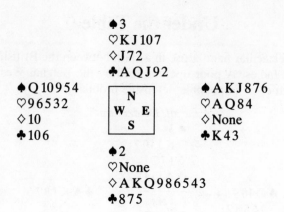

♠3
♡KJ107
◇J72
♣AQJ92

♠Q10954
♡96532
◇10
♣106

♠AKJ876
♡AQ84
◇None
♣K43

♠2
♡None
◇AKQ986543
♣875

To beat the slam East must make the super return of a *low* heart. Declarer can discard one club but no further trick can be established in the heart suit and a club trick must eventually be lost. (A spade at trick two is not good enough; declarer can ruff in dummy and establish a heart winner.)

Since at most one spade trick would stand up, West would have done better to lead the *queen* of spades. Then a switch to either clubs or hearts would beat the contract.

In the other room the British East-West took out insurance in six spades doubled over six diamonds. After a club lead to the ace, North understandably returned a diamond rather than a heart. When declarer subsequently led a heart from dummy North played safe by inserting an honour and the defenders collected only 200.

Look the Other Way

The play of this deal from the final of a big event in America was widely reported at the time. It is a fine example of a form of play that very few would recognise.

Game all; Dealer South.

```
              ♠ Q 6 2
              ♡ 10 9 8 7 4 2
              ◇ J 8 5
              ♣ 7
♠ K 10 8 7              ♠ A J 9 5 4 3
♡ Q J 3        N        ♡ A K 5
◇ 4 3        W   E      ◇ 10 9 2
♣ K Q 10 8     S        ♣ 2
              ♠ None
              ♡ 6
              ◇ A K Q 7 6
              ♣ A J 9 6 5 4 3
```

West	North	East	South
Wolff	*Cohen*	*Hamman*	*Bergen*
			1♣
Pass	1♡	2♠	3◇
4♠	Pass	Pass	4NT[1]
Pass	5◇	Double	All Pass

[1] Not Blackwood but unusual no-trump, indicating that he wanted to compete in one of his suits.

West led a low spade, East put in the jack and South ruffed. Declarer cashed the ace of clubs and followed with a second club, ruffed by the eight of diamonds, which East, as you see, can overruff. What do you suppose was the result — one down, two down, three down?

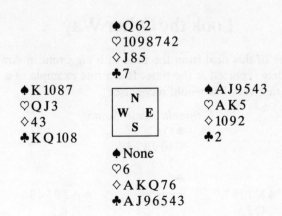

```
                      ♠ Q 6 2
                      ♡ 1098742
                      ♢ J 8 5
                      ♣ 7
    ♠ K 1087                        ♠ A J 9 5 4 3
    ♡ Q J 3          N              ♡ A K 5
    ♢ 4 3          W   E            ♢ 1092
    ♣ K Q 108        S              ♣ 2
                      ♠ None
                      ♡ 6
                      ♢ A K Q 7 6
                      ♣ A J 9 6 5 4 3
```

Suppose that East overruffs and forces again in spades.
South can ruff a third club with the jack of diamonds, draw
trumps in two rounds, and give up a club. He still has a
trump and is only one down, having lost an overruff, a club,
and a heart.

But Hamman did *not* overruff at trick three; he discarded
a low heart, following the general principle that when the
declarer is negotiating a two-suiter it is usually right to
conserve one's trumps.

If you try various lines of play now you will find that declarer
will never get his clubs going. At best, as at the table, he will
make five diamond tricks in hand, two ruffs (with the eight
and jack of diamonds), and just the ace of clubs. That was
three down, 800. At the other table the declarer in the same
contract, against a different lead, was two down, 500. The
brilliant defence of not overruffing the eight of diamonds
therefore led to a gain of 7 IMPs instead of a loss of seven.

Part 7

Comic Cuts

As everyone knows, our game gives rise to many
comical happenings.

Well-placed Queen

In November 1948 the Second American Zone Championship was held in Heidelberg, Germany (where many Americans were stationed). In the final of the teams the relatively unknown pairing of Mr and Mrs Gotthelf recorded a notable triumph on this deal:

East-West game; Dealer East.

```
              ♠ K 107432
              ♡ 2
              ◇ Q 109
              ♣ A K 8
  ♠ A 85          N          ♠ Q 6
  ♡ 864      W       E       ♡ A Q J 53
  ◇ A J 5        S           ◇ 872
  ♣ J 742                    ♣ Q 106
              ♠ J 9
              ♡ K 1097
              ◇ K 643
              ♣ 953
```

West	North	East	South
Adler	*Mr Gotthelf*	*Hahn*	*Mrs Gotthelf*
		1♡	1♠
Pass	3♠	Pass	3 NT
Pass	4♠	Pass	Pass
Double	All Pass		

The bidding may seem unorthodox by today's standards but there is in fact a logical — well, semi-logical — explanation for it. First, South was not paying much attention at the time and was under the impression that her husband had dealt and opened one club. She said later that her spade bid was an attempt to avoid a spade lead in an eventual no-trump contract. Despite the fact that his wife was no star at dummy play, Mr Gotthelf thought that his six trumps, an ace-king and a singleton justified a double raise in spades. Mrs G, whose hand did not seem to offer much potential for suit play, took refuge in three no-trumps, but Mr G still had confidence in his trump support.

West, showing no respect for this thoughtful sequence, closed the auction with a double and led a heart. How do you think the redoubtable Mrs G fulfilled her contract?

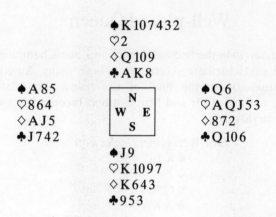

♠ K 107432
♡ 2
◇ Q 109
♣ A K 8

♠ A 85
♡ 864
◇ A J 5
♣ J 742

N
W   E
S

♠ Q 6
♡ A Q J 53
◇ 872
♣ Q 106

♠ J 9
♡ K 1097
◇ K 643
♣ 953

West led a heart against four spades doubled. East won with
the ace and returned the queen of hearts, taken by declarer's
king. There were three aces to lose, so declarer could not
afford to lose to the jack of diamonds or queen of spades.
Her first move was a diamond to the ten. She hoped that this
card would force the ace and that she would subsequently be
able to return to the king of diamonds for a spade finesse. In
fact the ten of diamonds held the trick and Mrs G was stuck
in the dummy. Casually she led a low trump. East made the
'natural' play of ducking and from then on it was plain sailing.
The jack forced the ace and the king subsequently dropped
the queen.

So, West learnt his lesson. It just shows how easy it is to
underestimate the bidding of unknown opponents.

No Way Home

Two husband-and-wife combinations faced each other at a crucial stage of a match in the 1956 Hubert Phillips Bowl (mixed teams, aggregate scoring). This was the deciding board:

Game all; Dealer South.

```
              ♠ K 7 6 4
              ♡ 1 0 8 3
              ◇ A J 2
              ♣ A Q 3
♠ Q 1 0 5 2                    ♠ J 9
♡ 5 4           N             ♡ J 6 2
◇ None       W     E          ◇ 1 0 9 8 5 3
♣ K J 8 7 6 4 2   S           ♣ 1 0 9 5
              ♠ A 8 3
              ♡ A K Q 9 7
              ◇ K Q 7 6 4
              ♣ None
```

West	North	East	South
			2♡
Pass	3♡	Pass	4 NT
Pass	5♡	Pass	5 NT
Pass	6◇	Pass	7♡
All Pass			

West led a spade and declarer saw that all would depend on a reasonable lie in the trump suit. She cashed the ace of trumps and, with bated breath, continued with the king. When both defenders followed, she tabled her cards with a triumphant "There they are!"

Mutual congratulations in the North-South plane were interrupted when East declared that he was not entirely happy with the claim.

"I naturally play another round of trumps," said South, with a sinking feeling.

"Naturally," echoed North.

At this time the Laws were severe on the subject. Since at the time of the claim South had not indicated her intention to draw the outstanding trump, she was not allowed (unless she had no alternative) to lead trumps while either defender had a trump.

What do you think the effect of this ruling was?

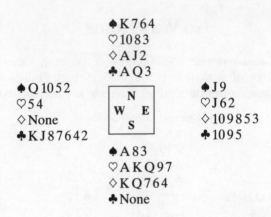

```
                 ♠ K764
                 ♡ 1083
                 ◇ A J 2
                 ♣ A Q 3
♠ Q 1052                          ♠ J 9
♡ 54          N                   ♡ J 62
◇ None    W       E               ◇ 109853
♣ K J 87642       S               ♣ 1095
                 ♠ A 83
                 ♡ A K Q 97
                 ◇ K Q 764
                 ♣ None
```

Prohibited from pulling the last trump, South turned to the diamond suit. A frustrated East had to follow to five rounds, the last of which was ruffed in dummy. Two more winners in the black suits followed, after which declarer was down to all trumps and could at last draw the outstanding trump. Thirteen tricks made.

Would South have made her contract if the defenders had not enforced the penalty? She would have drawn the last trump, no doubt. When the diamond loser becomes apparent, a possible line is to discard a spade on the ace of clubs and play to ruff the thirteenth spade good. Spades are not 3–3, so that line would fail. The other possibility is a black-suit squeeze on West. Since West has shown up with so few cards in the red suits, the squeeze is the better prospect. As it happens, though, declarer had actually won the spade lead with dummy's king. She would therefore have had no route home after drawing a third round of trumps.

Desperate Recovery

In 1959 a big rubber bridge event was organised in Monte Carlo. Claude Reichenbach suffered quite an adventure when he was sitting South with these cards:

♠J
♡KJ109765
♢J3
♣J72

It was Love All and his partner opened one club. "I'll show the type with a jump to three hearts," thought Claude, and when East overcalled with two diamonds he bid three hearts, as planned. Too late, he realised that three hearts over two diamonds had the ring of a standard force. The auction proceeded in nightmare fashion:

West	North	East	South
	Babovitch		*Reichenbach*
	1♣	2♢	3♡
4♠	5♢¹	6♣²	6♡³
6♠	Double	Pass	?

¹ Cue-bid, agreeing hearts.
² Cue-bid, agreeing spades!
³ 'Maybe partner will realise that I'm not keen to defend against spades — that I'd prefer to play in hearts'.

What would you do now? Would you pass, hoping that six spades will go down, or would you sacrifice in seven hearts?

Reichenbach decided to sacrifice. His call of seven hearts was doubled by West, ending the auction. This was the complete deal:

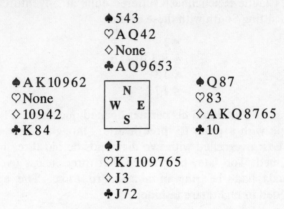

```
                      ♠543
                      ♡AQ42
                      ◇None
                      ♣AQ9653
   ♠AK10962                        ♠Q87
   ♡None           N               ♡83
   ◇10942       W     E            ◇AKQ8765
   ♣K84            S               ♣10
                      ♠J
                      ♡KJ109765
                      ◇J3
                      ♣J72
```

West had a tough problem with his opening lead. Should he lead partner's suit or his own? Just in time he recalled that at some point East had cue-bid clubs, obviously indicating a lead. West flicked the eight of clubs onto the table.

Reichenbach played low from dummy and soon wrapped up thirteen tricks. At rubber-bridge scoring this was quite a profitable sacrifice.

Funny Peculiar

This hand is from a pairs championship in France. Almost anything might happen and most things did.

North-South game; Dealer North.

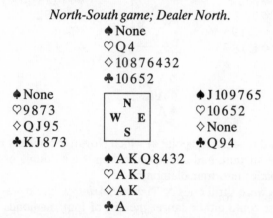

North:
♠ None
♡ Q 4
◇ 10876432
♣ 10652

West:
♠ None
♡ 9873
◇ Q J 9 5
♣ K J 8 7 3

East:
♠ J 109765
♡ 10652
◇ None
♣ Q 9 4

South:
♠ A K Q 8 4 3 2
♡ A K J
◇ A K
♣ A

One South player was so excited by his holding that he opened two clubs out of turn. The auction reverted to North, who passed, and East then opened three spades. It was, of course, silly to pre-empt when one of the opponents (North) was barred from the auction. South, happy in the knowledge that his partner could not speak, examined his hand carefully and doubled three spades. West passed and North uttered "Four diamonds".

"Sacré bleu!" exclaimed South. "You are not allowed to bid."

"That's not for you to say," put in West, well pleased by this latest turn of events. "You can condone the illegal call if you want to, partner."

It is hardly a fair question, but what do you suppose happened next?

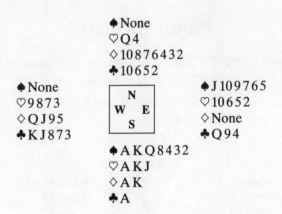

♠ None
♡ Q 4
◇ 10876432
♣ 10652

♠ None
♡ 9873
◇ Q J 95
♣ K J 873

♠ J 109765
♡ 10652
◇ None
♣ Q 94

♠ A K Q 8432
♡ A K J
◇ A K
♣ A

We had reached the point at which North, technically barred from the auction, had attempted to remove a double of East's three spades into four diamonds.

There were shrill cries of '*Arbitre! Arbitre!*' and it was ruled that East could either cancel the bid of four diamonds or let it stand. Confused by the clamour, East made the uninspired choice to play in three spades doubled and lost 900 (which today would be 1100).

This was the best result for any North-South pair and the next best was obtained in a curious way by a bright spark who opened seven no-trumps on the South cards. When West led a diamond, East discarded a spade. "I'll try that again," thought South, and on the next diamond East discarded another spade. It was a disappointment now to find that the suit was still guarded, but one down gave South an excellent score.

Opponents Were Ruthless

Bridge writers get odd letters from time to time. One of us had a query from a correspondent who, wondering whether to advance over her partner's five diamond response to four no-trumps, decided not to go for the slam and inadvertently passed five diamonds. She went on, "I explained I had made a mistake, but my opponents did not allow me to change my call to five spades, which was our suit. They had most of the diamonds and I was down three tricks."

The only solace it was possible to give her was that a similar misnomer once occurred in a world championship match.

Love all; Dealer North.

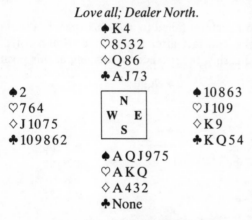

```
                ♠K4
                ♡8532
                ◇Q86
                ♣AJ73
 ♠2                          ♠10863
 ♡764         N              ♡J109
 ◇J1075     W   E            ◇K9
 ♣109862       S            ♣KQ54
                ♠AQJ975
                ♡AKQ
                ◇A432
                ♣None
```

The Argentine pair sitting North-South bid as follows:

South	North
	Pass
2♠	3♠
4◇	5◇
5NT	6◇
6♡	Pass (!)

North thought about bidding seven spades, decided not to, and passed. As great luck would have it, six hearts was on.

At the other table the Italian South played in six spades against a club lead. Ought he to make this, do you think?

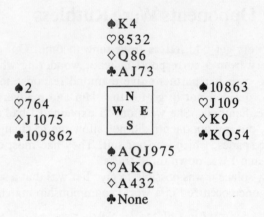

The Italian declarer failed to make six spades, although best play wins this contract after a club lead. South ruffs, draws trumps, and cashes the top hearts, arriving at this position:

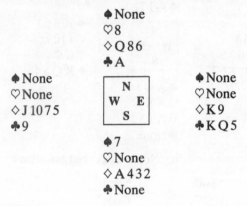

Declarer plays ace and another diamond. If he puts in the queen, no matter, because East will have only clubs left and South will obtain two discards, one on the ace of clubs and one the thirteenth heart.

From the Other Side

Purveyors of psychic bids have all but been hounded out of the game. A sign of the times is that the English Bridge Union has banned the long-standing Drury Convention (two clubs by a passed hand over partner's one heart or one spade opening) on the grounds that the convention *might* be used as a cover for psychic bids. Back in the 60s opening psychics were an accepted part of the game. Indeed when Yorkshire faced London in the 1961 Tollemache final *both* West players, first to speak at favourable vulnerability, opened one spade on this modest collection:

♠973
♡864
◇942
♣J742

At one table the auction then followed this path:

West	North	East	South
Tarlo		*Franklin*	
1♠	Double	2♣	3NT
Pass	Pass	Double	Pass
?			

What would you do now on the West cards? Stick to your guns or run to four clubs?

This was the full deal:

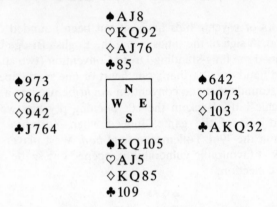

```
              ♠ A J 8
              ♡ K Q 9 2
              ◇ A J 7 6
              ♣ 8 5
♠ 9 7 3                      ♠ 6 4 2
♡ 8 6 4        N             ♡ 1 0 7 3
◇ 9 4 2     W     E          ◇ 1 0 3
♣ J 7 6 4      S             ♣ A K Q 3 2
              ♠ K Q 10 5
              ♡ A J 5
              ◇ K Q 8 5
              ♣ 10 9
```

Louis Tarlo, sitting West, ran to four clubs. This was doubled and went 900 down. Harold Franklin pointed out to his partner — in a very reasonable tone, of course — that after a vulnerable double and a three no-trumps response by the opponents an East player of the most *limited* intelligence would be able to deduce that West had psyched. It followed, in his humble opinion, that West should have left in the double. Louis replied — in an equally reasonable tone — that if his partner had passed three no-trumps his side would have scored an effortless 50 points instead of minus 900.

This was the auction in the other room:

West	North	East	South
Schapiro		*Rodrigue*	
1♠	1 NT	Double	Redouble
2♣	Pass	Pass	3 NT
All Pass			

Rodrigue saw no need to double the final contract. This was well judged, since if the opponents had run to game in spades, hearts or diamonds, they would have had an easy task there. Neither did Rodrigue have any problem in deciding which of partner's 'suits' to lead! He cashed the ace and king of clubs, then played a low club to avoid blocking the suit. That was one down and a big swing to London, the eventual winners.

Last Drop of Blood

What is the worst penalty that can follow a small misjudgement? East, on this deal from a match in Spain, could tell you.

Game all; Dealer South.

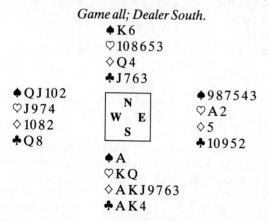

```
              ♠ K 6
              ♡ 10 8 6 5 3
              ◇ Q 4
              ♣ J 7 6 3
♠ Q J 10 2                    ♠ 9 8 7 5 4 3
♡ J 9 7 4        N           ♡ A 2
◇ 10 8 2      W   E          ◇ 5
♣ Q 8            S           ♣ 10 9 5 2
              ♠ A
              ♡ K Q
              ◇ A K J 9 7 6 3
              ♣ A K 4
```

North-South were playing one of the modern styles whereby two diamonds in response to two clubs promises an ace and two hearts is the negative. South forgot about this at first and the bidding went:

West	North	East	South
			2♣
Pass	2♡	Pass	3◇
Pass	3♡	Pass	7♡[1]
Pass	Pass	Double[2]	7NT
All Pass			

[1] He thinks his partner has made a positive response in hearts and has rebid the suit.

[2] Pretty silly, really, when one down undoubled will net a huge swing.

East thought that his final pass might persuade his partner to lead a heart, but West began with the queen of spades. What then?

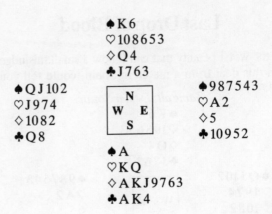

♠K6
♡108653
♢Q4
♣J763

♠QJ102　　♠987543
♡J974　　　♡A2
♢1082　　　♢5
♣Q8　　　　♣10952

♠A
♡KQ
♢AKJ9763
♣AK4

You can see what happened after the spade lead against seven no-trumps. South made two spades (discarding the king of hearts), two clubs, and six diamonds, to arrive at this position:

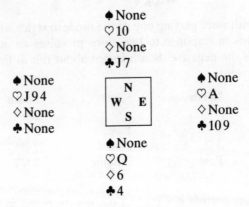

♠None
♡10
♢None
♣J7

♠None　　　♠None
♡J94　　　 ♡A
♢None　　　♢None
♣None　　　♣109

♠None
♡Q
♢6
♣4

On the last diamond East bid a final farewell to the ace of hearts.

Make Believe

If you want a lie to be believed, make it a big one. That was the theme of this deal from the team event at the Common Market Championship one year.

Love all; Dealer South.

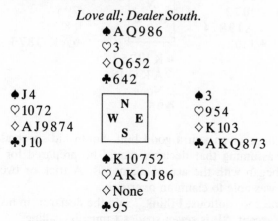

♠AQ986
♡3
◇Q652
♣642

♠J4
♡1072
◇AJ9874
♣J10

♠3
♡954
◇K103
♣AKQ873

♠K10752
♡AKQJ86
◇None
♣95

What would you open on the South hand? One heart, maybe, or perhaps a gun-crashing four hearts. (At rubber bridge there is much to be said for that sort of bid.) The Dutch player, Joop Van der Goot, chose one spade; not a bad idea; if by any chance partner can support spades you will be well placed. And this is what happened, for the bidding continued:

West	North	East	South
			1♠
Pass	4♠	5♣	?

What do you suppose South bid now, and with what result?

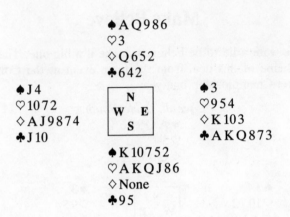

```
                  ♠ A Q 9 8 6
                  ♡ 3
                  ◇ Q 6 5 2
                  ♣ 6 4 2
♠ J 4          ┌─────────┐          ♠ 3
♡ 1 0 7 2      │   N     │          ♡ 9 5 4
◇ A J 9 8 7 4  │ W     E │          ◇ K 1 0 3
♣ J 1 0        │   S     │          ♣ A K Q 8 7 3
               └─────────┘
                  ♠ K 1 0 7 5 2
                  ♡ A K Q J 8 6
                  ◇ None
                  ♣ 9 5
```

We have given you a good hint. South bid six spades and West, assuming that declarer would be prepared for a club lead, began with the ace of diamonds. A trick or two later, South was able to claim an overtrick.

"I was too cautious, I think," said the declarer, in his heavy Dutch accent. "It is seven spades I must be calling."

This is not the first time that a coup of this nature has been reported from a big event. In a pre-war European Championship a Hungarian player, after a competitive auction, bid *seven* although holding a loser in the suit bid defensively by the opposition. Then, too, the defenders did not lead this suit and the grand slam was made. Maybe it's something we should try more often!

Take Fright

During British trials for the European Championship at Oslo in 1969 the East player on one deal held:

♠872
♡KJ92
◇1095
♣863

North-South were vulnerable and the bidding began as follows:

West	North	East	South
			1◇
3♡	5♠	?	

The natural interpretation of North's five spades is that he is asking his partner to bid six if he has one of the two top honours in spades, and seven if he holds ♠AK (or perhaps ♠AQ).

At this point what action would you take on the East hand?

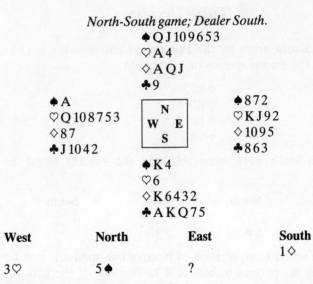

North-South game; Dealer South.

```
              ♠ Q J 109653
              ♡ A 4
              ◇ A Q J
              ♣ 9
♠ A                          ♠ 872
♡ Q 108753        N          ♡ K J 92
◇ 87           W     E       ◇ 1095
♣ J 1042          S          ♣ 863
              ♠ K 4
              ♡ 6
              ◇ K 6432
              ♣ A K Q 75
```

West	North	East	South
			1◇
3♡	5♠	?	

Now John Pugh, playing with Freddie North, made an interesting call; he doubled five spades! Not too brightly, South passed and North recorded an inadequate 1050. The double was of the variety known as 'stripe-tailed ape', because the doubler intends to flee like a stripe-tailed ape if there is a redouble.

At another table Priday and Rodrigue had the misfortune to arrive at seven spades on the North-South cards and the further misfortune to do so while Boris Schapiro was watching. "Tony and Claude had one unlucky hand," he assured everyone he met during the next two days. "They bid seven spades and the ace of trumps was on the wrong side."

The championship at Oslo that year was won by the Italians. The telex machine had a moment of empathy when reporting one of Ireland's matches: 'At half-time the Irish led by one pint.'

Forgotten Brief

In the 1986 Lederer Memorial Trophy the Journalists' team included the previously untried partnership of Rixi Markus and David Bird.

"Now, some of them will be playing this ridiculous Multi," warned the senior half of the partnership. "Over that we play that a double shows diamonds."

The tournament had not been long under way when the Journalists met Ireland. Bird, sitting East, held this hand, vulnerable against not:

♠ A K Q 9 8 2
♡ K 3
◇ K 10 7 4
♣ A

After two passes the Irishman to his right opened two diamonds, the Multi. Bird doubled, the normal first move on a good hand, and remembered two seconds later that this was meant to show diamonds. Ah well, king-ten to four was better than none at all.

"Two spades," said the next Irishman, indicating some support for hearts but little or none for spades.

A pass from Rixi was followed by a pass from the opener, implying that he held a weak two in spades. What would you do now?

This was the full deal:

East-West game; Dealer South.

```
                    ♠ None
                    ♡ A Q 9 8 4
                    ◇ 9 8 3 2
                    ♣ 10 9 7 4
    ♠ J 7 6 4 3              ┌─────────┐              ♠ A K Q 9 8 2
    ♡ 10 5                   │    N    │              ♡ K 3
    ◇ 5                      │  W   E  │              ◇ K 10 7 4
    ♣ K J 8 6 5              │    S    │              ♣ A
                            └─────────┘
                    ♠ 10 5
                    ♡ J 7 6 2
                    ◇ A Q J 6
                    ♣ Q 3 2
```

West	North	East	South
Markus	*Fitzgibbon*	*Bird*	*Mesbur*
			Pass
Pass	2◇	Double	2♠
Pass	Pass [1]	?	

[1] This was smart. He knew, of course, that the opponents had a vulnerable game in spades.

East feared that a further double might attract a three club response, after which a bid of three spades would be ambiguous to say the least. Deciding to take an undoubled penalty, he passed. West led a diamond and the appearance of the dummy caused a certain amount of mirth from North and South, mixed reactions from elsewhere. Declarer won East's king with the ace, took a losing heart finesse, and made no further trick (East's second heart going away on West's king of clubs). +350 for East-West.

At the other table this was the auction:

West	North	East	South
Senior	*Priday*	*Walshe*	*Simpson*
			Pass
Pass	2♡	4♠	5♡
5♠	Pass	6♠	All Pass

The defenders took their two aces to put the slam one down.

"Plus 100 on the next one," announced Priday when scores were compared.

"Plus 350," said Rixi.

"Ah, well done," replied Priday. "10 IMPs to us."

No Trouble at All

In 1990 a team loosely described as 'London' was invited to the Proton Inter-City tournament in Taipei. They narrowly failed to qualify for the final, but a few extra points from this deal against a local side would have been enough.

Take Irving Rose's hand. He was sitting West at favourable vulnerability and held these cards:

♠ 10 9 8 7 6 5 2
♡ 6
♢ K J 2
♣ 7 6

There was a pass in front of him and he opened three diamonds. A moment of madness? No, this call showed a pre-empt in one or other major. (Rose later described his suit as 'seven solid, missing the A K Q J').

Now the nightmare started. North, the next player, overcalled four spades! Silverstone, Rose's partner, bid five hearts, doubtless assuming that Rose's suit was hearts. The next player joined in with six clubs. This had been the bidding:

West	North	East	South
Rose		*Silverstone*	
			Pass
3♢	4♠	5♡	6♣
?			

What would you do now?

Rose could not bear the prospect of his partner sacrificing in six hearts. He therefore doubled six clubs, hoping that two defensive tricks might materialise. North's redouble closed the auction. This was the full deal:

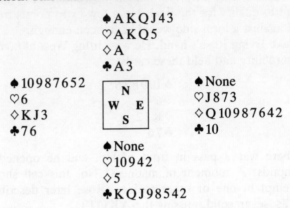

```
                    ♠ A K Q J 4 3
                    ♡ A K Q 5
                    ◇ A
                    ♣ A 3
   ♠ 10 9 8 7 6 5 2        N          ♠ None
   ♡ 6                W        E      ♡ J 8 7 3
   ◇ K J 3                S          ◇ Q 10 9 8 7 6 4 2
   ♣ 7 6                              ♣ 10
                    ♠ None
                    ♡ 10 9 4 2
                    ◇ 5
                    ♣ K Q J 9 8 5 4 2
```

Rose led his singleton heart and declarer immediately claimed the redoubled slam with an overtrick. "How much does that come to?" he said.

"2230," replied Rose, always very quick in such matters. "480 below, 100 for the insult, 400 for the overtrick, 750 for the slam and 500 for game."

Rose's team-mates, Tony Forrester and Andy Robson, soon arrived to compare scores. "Plus 2220," said Forrester, who had made seven no-trumps on the fateful board.

"Flat board," said Rose.

"Did they have any trouble with it?" enquired Forrester.

"None at all." replied Rose. "What did you do on the next one?"

Part 8

Dramatic Endings

One of these, as you will see, was of a different
character from the rest.

Question of Morale

Complete two-suiters are very rare, though we have met one or two in this book. Usually computer-dealing gets the blame, but this one occurred in the late 1950s before computers, if indeed they existed, had any employment in bridge events.

The deal below occurred at a critical point in the European Championship when Italy and France were in contention for first place.

East-West game; Dealer West.

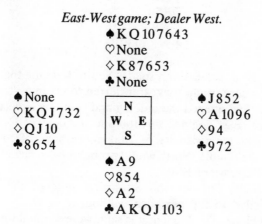

```
              ♠ K Q 10 7 6 4 3
              ♡ None
              ◇ K 8 7 6 5 3
              ♣ None
♠ None              N           ♠ J 8 5 2
♡ K Q J 7 3 2   W     E         ♡ A 10 9 6
◇ Q J 10            S            ◇ 9 4
♣ 8 6 5 4                        ♣ 9 7 2
              ♠ A 9
              ♡ 8 5 4
              ◇ A 2
              ♣ A K Q J 10 3
```

West	North	East	South
Jais	*Forquet*	*Trezel*	*Siniscalco*
1♡	4♠	Pass	4NT
Pass	6◇	Pass	6♠
Pass	7♠	Double	

Showing no respect for the Italian maestros, Trezel doubled the grand slam. What do you suppose happened then?

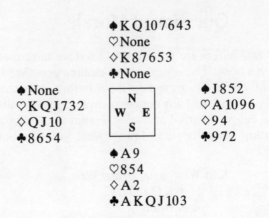

♠ K Q 10 7 6 4 3
♡ None
♢ K 8 7 6 5 3
♣ None

♠ None
♡ K Q J 7 3 2
♢ Q J 10
♣ 8 6 5 4

♠ J 8 5 2
♡ A 10 9 6
♢ 9 4
♣ 9 7 2

♠ A 9
♡ 8 5 4
♢ A 2
♣ A K Q J 10 3

When East doubled seven spades South, thinking that East must have a sure trump trick, transferred to seven no-trumps. His partner had opened the bidding and could be expected to hold an ace. East doubled this too and the defence took the first six tricks for a penalty of 1100 (more now, of course). In view of the double, North would probably have made seven spades, for a score of 1770.

The Italians, Forquet and Siniscalco, entered the score and proceeded to the next deal without a word or even a reproachful look. The French, it is said, were so dumbfounded by this superhuman restraint that they lost their nerve, the match and championship.

No Appeal

The Olympiad at Turin in 1960, the first of its kind, developed at the end into a struggle between Britain and France. In Britain's last match, against one of the three American teams (the system is different now), North-South were vulnerable and East held:

> ♠ A 8 7 6 5 2
> ♡ 9 7 3
> ♢ A 8 6 4
> ♣ None

South was the dealer and the bidding proceeded in this fashion:

West	North	East	South
			1♡
2♣	2 NT	Pass	3 NT
4♣	4♡	?	

Sitting East, you have not spoken so far. What would you bid now?

North-South game; Dealer South.

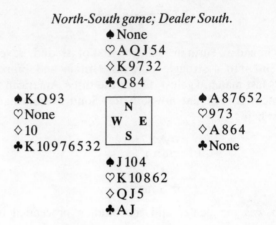

```
                ♠ None
                ♡ A Q J 5 4
                ◇ K 9 7 3 2
                ♣ Q 8 4
♠ K Q 9 3           N           ♠ A 8 7 6 5 2
♡ None          W       E       ♡ 9 7 3
◇ 10                S           ◇ A 8 6 4
♣ K 10 9 7 6 5 3 2              ♣ None
                ♠ J 10 4
                ♡ K 10 8 6 2
                ◇ Q J 5
                ♣ A J
```

West	North	East	South
Schapiro	*Ogust*	*Reese*	*Schenken*
			1♡
2♣	2NT[1]	Pass	3NT
4♣	4♡	Double[2]	Pass
Pass[3]	Pass		

[1] This, though nothing was said, was forcing and so, in a way, a controlled psychic.

[2] The obvious call, surely; he holds two aces and is void in the suit that partner has bid.

[3] Some critics said that West should have tried four spades now, but really, that is ridiculous. It looks to him as though his partner will have trump tricks.

After a spade lead South made two overtricks, while East-West could have made thirteen tricks in spades. (The declarer at the other table muddled the play in five spades and went one down.)

In those days players did not come to the table with a booklet describing their methods. The British captain might have claimed a foul, but this would have been desperately inconvenient for everyone on the last day and would not have changed the result — 1st France, 2nd Great Britain.

Fighting Finish

This deal from the qualifying round of a big team event in Miami had the bridgerama audience in the proverbial fits of laughter; those, at any rate, who were supporting the home side.

Game all; Dealer South.

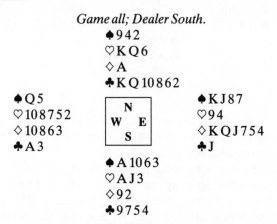

♠942
♥KQ6
♦A
♣KQ10862

♠Q5
♥108752
♦10863
♣A3

♠KJ87
♥94
♦KQJ754
♣J

♠A1063
♥AJ3
♦92
♣9754

The match between a top American and a top Indonesian team was level 55-55 when the last board was shown on the screen. The Indonesians in the closed room were shown to have lost 100 in five clubs. It looked now as though the Americans were going to pick up points in defence against a diamond contract, but they 'came again' and reached four spades on the North-South cards.

The commentators noted that South, playing for trumps to be 4–2, would probably go one down (three spades and a club), for a tied match. However, West made the imaginative lead of the three of clubs through dummy's suit. Can you guess what happened then?

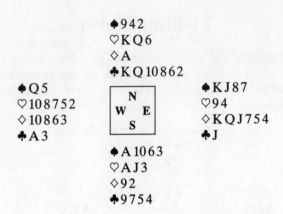

```
                        ♠942
                        ♡KQ6
                        ◇A
                        ♣KQ10862
        ♠Q5                           ♠KJ87
        ♡108752          N            ♡94
        ◇10863         W   E          ◇KQJ754
        ♣A3              S            ♣J
                        ♠A1063
                        ♡AJ3
                        ◇92
                        ♣9754
```

West, you will recall, led a low club against four spades. Dummy won and followed with the king of clubs. East *ruffed*, so now four spades was made.

This affair was described in the French magazine, which recounted another story against itself, as it were. In one of the pairs events the French international, Gérard Desrousseaux, arriving at a new table, began to describe his methods in English. His opponents listened politely for a few moments, then one of them ventured to interrupt him. "Sorry, sir," he said. "We don't speak French."

Strike Back

A powerful Italian squad won the 1969 European Championships. In the first half of their match against Sweden, they suffered several unlucky boards and were 62-17 down at half-time. They were out for blood when the second half started.

Game all; Dealer South.

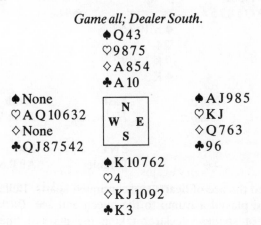

♠ Q 4 3
♡ 9 8 7 5
♢ A 8 5 4
♣ A 10

♠ None
♡ A Q 10 6 3 2
♢ None
♣ Q J 8 7 5 4 2

♠ A J 9 8 5
♡ K J
♢ Q 7 6 3
♣ 9 6

♠ K 10 7 6 2
♡ 4
♢ K J 10 9 2
♣ K 3

West	North	East	South
Bianchi	*Morback*	*Messina*	*Hall*
			1♠
4♡	Double	Redouble	All Pass

The Swedish North found a good opening lead, the diamond ace. Bianchi ruffed and set about his side suit, leading the jack of clubs. North rose with the ace and forced declarer with another diamond, reducing Bianchi to four trumps.

A second round of clubs went to South's king and back came the king of diamonds. Bianchi prudently discarded a club and nothing could now defeat the contract. +1030 to the Italians.

East doubtless thought that his redouble was safe, since if the opponents ran to four spades he would be able to deal with this in a big way. In the other room, though, Belladonna managed to make four spades doubled, after ace and another heart. Can you see how?

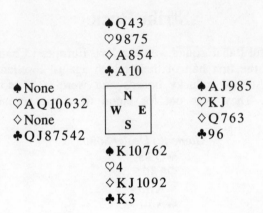

	♠ Q 43		
	♡ 9875		
	◇ A 854		
	♣ A 10		

(diagram)

♠ None   ♠ A J 985
♡ A Q 10632   ♡ K J
◇ None   ◇ Q 763
♣ Q J 87542   ♣ 96

♠ K 10762
♡ 4
◇ K J 1092
♣ K 3

West	North	East	South
Axelsson	*Garozzo*	*Holmgren*	*Belladonna*
			1♠
2♡	2♠	2NT	3♠
4♣	4♠	Double	All Pass

West led the ace of hearts and continued hearts. Belladonna ruffed and played a trump to the queen and ace. Back came the nine of spades, declarer taking the marked finesse of the ten.

Belladonna's next play was the *jack* of diamonds from hand. This was not a schoolboy attempt to 'find the lady'; it was an essential unblocking move. West showed out and dummy's ace won the trick. After three more diamonds and two clubs this was the position, with the lead in dummy:

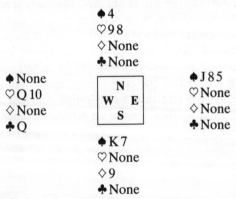

♠ 4
♡ 98
◇ None
♣ None

♠ None   ♠ J 85
♡ Q 10   ♡ None
◇ None   ◇ None
♣ Q   ♣ None

♠ K 7
♡ None
◇ 9
♣ None

Now a heart from dummy gave the Italians an 18 IMP swing. They eventually won the match 78-73.

No Marksman

What do you suppose was the most famous hand in bridge history? The Duke of Cumberland deal, where a grand slam was made against a hand containing 30 points? No, that was at whist, and the story may have been invented. But the historic tragedy that took place at the home of the Bennetts in Kansas City, Kansas, in 1931, will never be forgotten.

Game all; Dealer South.

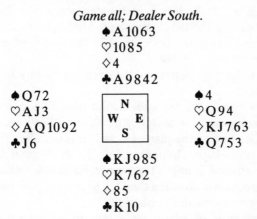

```
                ♠A1063
                ♡1085
                ◇4
                ♣A9842
♠Q72           ┌─────────┐        ♠4
♡AJ3           │    N    │        ♡Q94
◇AQ1092        │ W     E │        ◇KJ763
♣J6            │    S    │        ♣Q753
               └─────────┘
                ♠KJ985
                ♡K762
                ◇85
                ♣K10
```

The Bennetts were entertaining their friends, the Hoffmans. It was not exactly a 'Famous Match', for team tournaments had hardly begun at this time, but the weekly game was an important event for both couples.

No slave to the two-and-a-half quick tricks theory that was prevalent then, Mr Bennett opened one spade on the South cards and soon finished in four spades. Mr Hoffman, West, began with the ace of diamonds. Another diamond is best, weakening the hand with the long side suit, but Mr Hoffman switched to the jack of clubs. The contract can be made at double dummy now (three rounds of trumps, picking up the queen, then ace and nine of clubs), but Mr Bennett finished two down.

What do you think happened next?

"Aw, that sure was a bum play." stated Mrs Bennett, shifting her gum from one side to the other. A furious row followed. Bennett (said Mrs Hoffman later), reached across the table, grabbed his wife's arm and slapped her several times. Mrs Bennett repeated over and over again, "Nobody but a bum would hit a woman."

Declaring that he would spend the night elsewhere, Mr Bennett went upstairs to pack. A few moments later he was talking to Mr Hoffman in his den when Mrs Bennett appeared, waving the family revolver. Mr Bennett ran to the bathroom and locked the door, but Mrs Bennett fired through it twice and hit him — fatally.

"I've shot the guy. Better call the cops." cried Mrs Bennett, grief-stricken.

Ely Culbertson gave evidence at the trial. In a peroration obviously composed for posterity he stated, "We have heard of lives depending on the play of a card. It is not often that we find this figure of speech literally true . . . Mr Bennett started to pull the adverse trumps. Here again he flirted with death, as people frequently do when they fail to make a plan either in the game of bridge or the game of life."

The jury, most of whom were not bridge players, were subjected to a detailed analysis of the various possible lines of play. Culbertson's momentous address then drew mercifully to a close: "If West had played back a trump at this stage this might still have permitted the fatal denouement. But at least Mr Bennett would have died happy in the knowledge that he had played the cards dealt him by fate to the very best of his ability."

Mrs Bennett was acquitted on the charge of murder. Perhaps the jury agreed with her that her husband's line of play had been unacceptable. Or maybe the explanation lies in a remark by one of the jury to the pressmen: "She was only a woman, unused to guns. We reckoned that if she'd really been trying to hit him she would have missed."

Index of named players

Famous Hands
from Famous Matches

In the sixty odd years of tournament bridge there
have been innumerable brilliant, disastrous,
or mirth-provoking deals. The authors describe
some of the brightest and best, including at least one
that led to murder.
Many of the deals are clever, but not heavyweight:
they touch on the history and humour of the game.
In every case the scene is set on the first of two pages
and the reader is asked:
What do you suppose happened next?

Terence Reese is one of the world's most prolific and
instructive authors. As a player he had few equals;
his many successes include the World Championship of 1955
and
David Bird is best known for his highly entertaining Abbot
stories which have graced many of the world's
bridge magazines and several books. His witty and acerbic
writing style complements his co-author perfectly.